Energy flows where focus goes.

SAM PENNY
The Topify Method

topifymethod.com

Chips Investments Pty Ltd
Parcel Collect 10042 76215
Shop 4, 44 Landsborough Parade
Golden Beach QLD 4551 Australia

Chips Investments Pty Ltd is the publisher of this book. More information can be found at www.topifymethod.com.

Copyright © Sam Penny 2025 All rights reserved.

No part of this book may be reproduced, stored in a retrieval system, or transmitted in any form or by any means—electronic, mechanical, photocopying, recording, or otherwise—without prior written permission from the publisher, except for brief quotations used in a review or critical analysis.

A CIP catalogue record for this book is available from the National Library of Australia. ISBN 978-1-7638968-8-8

Design by Sam Penny

Chips Investments Pty Ltd is committed to sustainability. This book is printed on paper sourced from responsibly managed forests.

DEDICATION

For those looking for their next mountain to climb.

CONTENTS

Preface	8
The Topify Philosophy	10
The Power of Structured Action	10
Why Most Productivity Methods Fail	11
What Makes the Topify Method Different?	15
How This Book Will Change Your Approach to Achievement	18
Part 1: The Dream	22
Chapter 1: The Power of Thinking Big	24
Why You Need a Dream That Excites You	25
The Psychology of Big Goals	28
Avoiding the Trap of Small Thinking	32
Chapter 2: Clarity Over Chaos	38
Defining Your Vision with Precision	39
The Topify Vision Framework	44
Turning Vague Ideas into Actionable Clarity	48
Summary of Part 1: The Dream	54
From Vision to Reality: Unlocking the Power of Big Dreams	54
The Power of Thinking Big	54
The Psychology of Big Goals	55
Avoiding the Trap of Small Thinking	55
Turning Dreams into Clarity	56
Part 2: The Strategy	57
Chapter 3: Reverse Engineering Success	59
Breaking Big Goals into Actionable Steps	60
The 90-Day Sprint Approach	65
Designing a System That Works for You	70
Chapter 4: The Topify Quadrants	76

The Four Types of Action: Essential, Growth, Delegation, Elimination	77
The Simplicity of Prioritization: Choosing What Truly Matters	82
How to Cut the Noise and Focus on Impact	86

Chapter 5: The Science of Habit Stacking — 92

Building Non-Negotiable Daily Routines	93
Leveraging Momentum for Success	98
The Compound Effect of Small Actions	102

Summary of Part 2: The Strategy — 108

Reverse Engineering Success	108
The Topify Quadrants: Prioritizing What Truly Matters	108
The Science of Habit Stacking	109
The Compound Effect: How Small Actions Lead to Big Results	109

Part 3: The Execution — 111

Chapter 6: The Daily Plan That Wins — 113

Why a Daily Plan is Non-Negotiable	113
Designing Your Perfect Day with the Topify Productivity Planner	114
Morning Mindset, Action Blocks, and Review Cycles	119
The Difference Between Busy and Productive	124

Chapter 7: Overcoming Resistance — 131

The Psychology of Procrastination	132
Rewiring Your Brain for Execution	137
How to Win When Motivation Fails	142

Chapter 8: The 45-Second Reset — 148

The Topify Reflection Method	149
How Micro-Adjustments Drive Massive Success	153
The Evening Review That Locks in Progress	159

Summary: The Execution — 165

Turning Plans into Daily Success	165
Designing a Winning Day	165

The Topify Method

    Overcoming Resistance and Taking Action   166
    The 45-Second Reset and Continuous Refinement   166
    Locking in Progress with the Evening Review   167

Part 4: The Scaling Effect   168

Chapter 9: Mastering Focus in a Distracted World   170
    Eliminating Digital and Mental Clutter   171
    How to Create Deep Work Environments   174
    The Art of Saying No Without Guilt   180

Chapter 10: Leveraging Accountability & Feedback   185
    Why Accountability and Feedback Matter   185
    Why Self-Discipline Isn't Enough   186
    Building a Topify Circle of Accountability   190
    The Power of Public and Private Commitments   195

Chapter 11: Thinking Like a High Performer   201
    The Difference Between Average and Elite Execution   202
    Why Discomfort Is Your Greatest Advantage   214

Summary: The Scaling Effect   219
    Elevating Execution to the Next Level   219
    Mastering Focus in a Distracted World   219
    Leveraging Accountability and Feedback   219
    Thinking Like a High Performer   220
    The Scaling Effect in Action   220

Part 5: The Legacy   221
    Beyond Success—Building a Legacy   221
    The Transition from Productivity to Purpose   221
    The Topify Challenge: The Next Step in Mastery   221

Chapter 12: Turning Productivity into Purpose   223
    Beyond Productivity—Finding Meaning in Action   223
    Designing a Life That Aligns with Your Values   227
    Scaling Your Impact Beyond Personal Success   231

Chapter 13: The Topify Challenge — **236**
    The Ultimate Test of Execution — 236
    Implementing the Topify Method for 90 Days — 237
    The Topify Scorecard — 240
    Unlocking the Next Level of Your Life — 243

Summary: The Legacy — **249**
    Elevating Productivity into Purpose — 249
    Turning Productivity into Purpose — 249
    The Topify Challenge: The 90-Day Execution Plan — 249
    Unlocking the Next Level — 250
    The Final Shift: From Productivity to Legacy — 250

Your Future Starts Now — **251**
    The Power to Create Change — 251
    The Power of Intentional Execution — 252
    The Invitation to Join the Topify Movement — 256
    Turning Strategy into Execution — 260

Want More? Unlock Hidden Insights, Exclusive Content & Bonus Resources!

This Book Comes with a Secret Bonus!
Don't Miss Out!
Scan This Now & Join
Thousands
of Smart Readers!

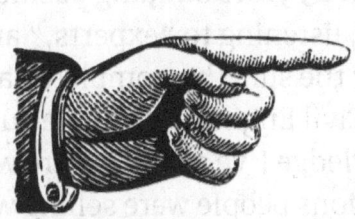

SCAN TO UNLOCK!

Preface

I remember standing on the edge of the water, staring out at the English Channel. Ready to swim the 34km to France. It was a dream come true. Most people train for years to take on this challenge, but I had only given myself 90 days. Ninety days to prepare my mind, my body, and my approach. And yet, as I took that first stroke into the dark, icy water, I knew I was going to make it. Not because I had all the answers. Not because I was the best swimmer. But because I had a simple, structured way of getting things done.

That's what this book is about.

For years, I've watched as people—entrepreneurs, athletes, professionals—struggle to turn their dreams into action. It's not because they aren't capable. It's not because they lack ambition. It's because everything is made too damn complicated. I know because I've been there.

I've spent more than 25 years building businesses and brands, attending seminars, listening to "experts," and reading about every process under the sun. I've completed an MBA, a Master's at MIT, and have a Civil Engineering degree under my belt. But despite all the knowledge I've gained, there was always one problem—the solutions people were selling were too complex. It doesn't have to be that way.

Life and business shouldn't be this hard. If you have a dream, you should have a clear and simple way to achieve it. That's why

I created The Topify Method. It's not about motivation, willpower, or completely overhauling your mindset. It's about action.

This book is packed with easy-to-apply methods that don't require deep self-exploration or soul-searching. You don't need to spend weeks reflecting on your purpose. You just need to start. Whether you want to grow your business, improve your fitness, or just get more out of life, this method will show you how to take the first step today—and then another, and another.

If you follow this book cover to cover, you'll see real change. If you share it with others, you'll help them do the same. My hope is that The Topify Method gives you the confidence to take small steps, every single day, toward the life you know you can achieve.

You don't need years of planning. You need 90 days and a system that works. If you can dream it, you can achieve it.

Sam Penny

The Topify Philosophy

The Power of Structured Action

What if everything you've ever dreamed of achieving wasn't just possible but inevitable? The difference between those who dream and those who execute lies in the ability to turn aspirations into structured, consistent action. That's where the Topify Method comes in.

For years, productivity systems have promised transformation but often fall short because they focus too much on rigid structures rather than adaptability. The Topify Method is different. It blends the science of peak performance with the psychology of motivation, helping you bridge the gap between ambition and execution.

This book is designed to take you from dream to daily action. It's not just about setting goals; it's about designing a system that ensures progress every single day. We'll guide you through the essential steps to clarify your vision, reverse-engineer success, master prioritization, and overcome obstacles that stand in your way.

By the time you finish this book, you will have a clear blueprint for achievement and the tools to implement the Topify Method in your own life. More importantly, you'll have shifted your mindset from one of passive goal-setting to an active, daily pursuit of excellence.

Are you ready to take control of your future? The journey starts now.

Why Most Productivity Methods Fail

Despite the abundance of productivity advice available, most methods fail because they are overly complicated, too rigid, or disconnected from real-life execution. Many systems prioritize organization over action, leaving people stuck in a cycle of planning rather than doing. The result? A feeling of productivity without real progress.

The Illusion of Productivity

Many people believe that being busy equates to being productive. They spend hours making elaborate to-do lists, setting up sophisticated project management tools, and reading countless self-help books—yet they fail to take meaningful, consistent action. The illusion of productivity keeps them occupied but prevents them from making actual progress toward their goals.

The Topify Method emphasizes execution over excessive planning. A structured yet flexible approach ensures that every step you take moves you closer to your goals, rather than getting lost in endless preparation.

Rigid Systems Fail in Real Life

Most productivity methods fail because they demand rigid adherence. Life is unpredictable, and any system that doesn't allow for flexibility leads to frustration and eventual abandonment. If a single missed task derails your progress, the system is setting you up for failure.

The Topify Method is different. It is adaptable. It allows for adjustments without losing momentum. Instead of focusing on a strict, unyielding framework, it encourages daily progress, even when circumstances change.

The Paralysis of Too Many Choices

With thousands of productivity apps, techniques, and systems available, people often feel overwhelmed by choices. They spend more time researching productivity hacks than actually implementing them. The paradox of choice leads to decision paralysis—the inability to commit to a single method because another seemingly better one might exist.

The key is simplicity. The Topify Method cuts through the noise and provides a straightforward, effective approach that anyone can follow without constantly second-guessing themselves.

The Myth of the Perfect Time

A major reason productivity methods fail is the belief that you need to wait for the "perfect time" to start. People tell themselves they'll begin when they have more time, more motivation, or better circumstances. This mindset delays action indefinitely.

The reality is that there is no perfect time. Action itself creates momentum, and the best way to start is to take small, consistent steps forward—right now.

Over-Reliance on Motivation

Many productivity systems rely on motivation as the driving force behind action. But motivation is fleeting. It fluctuates based on mood, energy levels, and external factors. If your productivity method depends on feeling inspired, you'll struggle to maintain progress on days when motivation is low.

The Topify Method removes motivation from the equation. Instead, it focuses on building habits, structure, and systems that make action automatic—even when you don't feel like it.

Complexity Kills Execution

Some productivity methods introduce unnecessary complexity, requiring multiple apps, elaborate workflows, and time-consuming reviews. The more complicated a system is, the less likely people are to stick with it.

Simplicity drives success. The Topify Method focuses on streamlining productivity into daily, repeatable habits that require minimal effort to maintain.

Measuring Progress Incorrectly

Many people track the wrong metrics when assessing their productivity. They measure hours worked, tasks completed, or time spent planning—but these don't necessarily equate to meaningful progress.

The Topify Method emphasizes results over activity. Instead of tracking arbitrary metrics, it focuses on outcomes that move the needle forward in your business, career, or personal life.

Lack of Accountability

Most productivity methods fail because they don't incorporate accountability. Without an external or internal system to keep you on track, it's easy to procrastinate and justify delays.

The Topify Method encourages both self-accountability and external accountability through structured reflection, progress tracking, and engagement with others who share your commitment to growth.

The Fix: A System That Works in the Real World

The Topify Method addresses these common pitfalls by providing a simple, flexible, and execution-driven system. It removes unnecessary complexity, eliminates reliance on motivation, and prioritizes daily progress over perfection.

In the following sections, we'll explore how to replace ineffective habits with a structured, results-driven framework that guarantees consistent progress toward your goals—without burnout or frustration.

By the end of this book, you'll have a productivity method that works for you, rather than forcing you to work within a rigid system that doesn't align with real life.

What Makes the Topify Method Different?

The Topify Method stands apart from traditional productivity approaches because it is designed with simplicity, adaptability, and execution in mind. It eliminates the complexity that often derails progress and replaces it with a clear, actionable system that is easy to implement and sustain.

1. Focus on Daily Action, Not Just Planning

Many productivity methods emphasize goal setting but neglect the daily execution required to achieve those goals. The Topify Method bridges that gap by ensuring that every day moves you forward in a tangible way. Instead of focusing on long-term aspirations without an execution plan, it helps you identify small, high-impact actions that compound over time.

2. Adaptability Over Rigidity

Life is unpredictable, and rigid systems break under pressure. The Topify Method is built to be flexible, allowing you to adjust while maintaining momentum. Whether you face unexpected challenges or need to shift priorities, the framework adapts without derailing your progress.

3. The Power of the 90-Day Sprint

Rather than setting vague, long-term goals, the Topify Method employs 90-day sprints—a focused, time-bound system that ensures consistent progress. Each sprint is broken down into:

- A clear outcome to achieve in 90 days
- Monthly milestones to track progress
- Weekly focus areas that drive momentum
- Daily tasks to ensure execution

This approach keeps motivation high and provides tangible results without overwhelming complexity.

4. Eliminating the Need for Motivation

Traditional productivity methods assume that you'll always be motivated to take action. The Topify Method removes this dependency by integrating structured habits that make action automatic. By designing your environment and routines to reduce decision fatigue, you can maintain momentum even on days when motivation is low.

5. Simplicity Drives Execution

Many productivity systems overwhelm users with complex tools and multiple layers of organization. The Topify Method is different—it is intentionally simple. By stripping away unnecessary elements, it allows you to focus only on what truly moves the needle forward.

6. Measurable Progress Over Busywork

Unlike traditional methods that track input-based metrics (e.g., hours worked, tasks completed), the Topify Method prioritizes output-based success. This means measuring results in terms of real-world progress, ensuring that each action contributes directly to your long-term vision.

7. Accountability at Every Level

Self-discipline alone isn't enough. The Topify Method integrates internal and external accountability mechanisms to keep you on track. Whether through self-reflection, structured review cycles, or leveraging a peer accountability system, you stay committed to your goals.

8. The Topify Reflection Cycle

Instead of blindly pushing forward, the Topify Method encourages continuous reflection and course correction. Each week, month, and 90-day sprint includes structured review sessions to identify wins, address roadblocks, and refine strategies.

9. Building a System That Works for YOU

The Topify Method isn't a one-size-fits-all system. It's a framework that you customize to fit your personal strengths, lifestyle, and ambitions. Whether you're an entrepreneur, an athlete, or someone looking to optimize their personal growth, it adapts to your needs.

10. The Key to Long-Term Success

Unlike methods that burn you out with unrealistic demands, the Topify Method is designed for sustainable success. By prioritizing balance, structured execution, and personal growth, it ensures that productivity becomes a way of life, not just a short-term effort.

How This Book Will Change Your Approach to Achievement

Achievement is not reserved for the exceptionally talented, the privileged, or those who have all the resources at their fingertips. Achievement is the result of consistent, purposeful action—and that's exactly what this book will help you master.

Most people fail to reach their true potential not because they lack ability, but because they lack a system that makes success inevitable. This book is designed to change that. It will rewire how you approach goal setting, execution, and progress—forever shifting your mindset from uncertainty to unstoppable momentum.

1. Shifting from Dreaming to Doing

Too many people spend their lives dreaming of what they want but never take the necessary steps to make it real. This book will show you how to convert aspirations into daily, achievable actions, making success a process rather than an abstract goal. By the end of this journey, you won't just dream—you will be in motion.

2. Developing an Unshakable Mindset

The most successful people in the world are not those who never face obstacles—they are those who refuse to let obstacles stop them. The Topify Method will retrain your brain to see setbacks as opportunities, helping you build resilience, confidence, and mental toughness. You will learn how to maintain focus and persistence even when the path gets difficult.

3. Making Progress Inevitable

Instead of waiting for motivation or inspiration to strike, this book will teach you how to build systems that make progress automatic. You will learn how to set up your days, weeks, and months in a way that ensures continuous movement toward your goals—without needing bursts of willpower.

4. Eliminating Overwhelm and Complexity

Many people get stuck because they overcomplicate their approach. This book will show you how to strip away the distractions, cut through the noise, and focus only on the actions that actually matter. You will discover how simplicity can lead to greater productivity and long-term results.

5. Creating Lasting Change

Most people make resolutions, start strong, and then quickly fall back into old habits. This book will teach you the science of habit formation—ensuring that once you establish momentum, it stays with you for life. You will no longer need to "start over" every few months; instead, you will build habits that last.

6. Unlocking the Power of Reflection and Adjustment

The key to sustained success is not just executing a plan—it's knowing how to adapt and refine your strategy as you grow. The Topify Method includes built-in reflection periods that allow you to assess what's working, make necessary tweaks, and keep your progress on track without frustration or burnout.

7. Aligning Your Actions with Your Purpose

Many people chase productivity for productivity's sake, but real fulfillment comes from aligning daily action with a deeper purpose. This book will help you identify what truly drives you so that your efforts are not just effective, but also deeply meaningful.

8. Building a Life of Achievement, Not Just a Moment of Success

True achievement is not about a single big win—it's about sustained excellence. The lessons in this book will help you not only achieve your goals but maintain success over time, preventing burnout and ensuring long-term fulfillment.

Final Thoughts: Your Journey Starts Now

This book is more than just a guide—it is a blueprint for lasting transformation. By the time you finish, you will no longer feel stuck, uncertain, or overwhelmed. Instead, you will have the tools, the mindset, and the strategy to execute on your biggest goals and turn achievement into a way of life.

The only thing left to do is begin. Let's get started.

Part 1: The Dream

Every great achievement begins as a dream. The world's most successful individuals, whether in business, sports, science, or the arts, started with a vision—an idea that ignited their passion and propelled them forward. But dreaming alone isn't enough. What separates those who achieve extraordinary things from those who remain stuck in mediocrity is the ability to transform dreams into structured, daily action.

The problem is that many people don't dream big enough. They allow fear, self-doubt, and societal conditioning to shrink their aspirations. They settle for what feels realistic rather than pushing the boundaries of possibility. The Topify Method challenges this mindset. It encourages you to embrace bold, audacious goals—the kind that excite and energize you.

However, having a dream isn't just about thinking big. It's about clarity. Many people have vague aspirations but struggle to define them in a way that makes achievement possible. Without clarity, dreams remain nothing more than wishful thinking.

This section of the book is designed to help you unlock the power of thinking big while also providing you with the tools to bring structure and focus to your vision. In Chapter 1, we will explore why dreaming big is essential, how ambitious goals shape your mindset, and how to avoid the common trap of small thinking. Then, in Chapter 2, we will dive into Clarity Over Chaos, where we break down the steps to refining your vision so that it becomes a concrete, actionable roadmap.

By the time you finish this section, you'll not only have a dream that excites you, but you'll also have the framework to turn that dream into a reality. Let's begin.

Chapter 1: The Power of Thinking Big

Everything you see around you was once just an idea. The greatest businesses, technological advancements, and artistic masterpieces all started with a single thought—an ambitious dream that someone dared to pursue. The ability to think big is not reserved for a select few; it is a skill that anyone can cultivate. And in this chapter, you will learn why embracing bold thinking is essential to unlocking your true potential.

Thinking big isn't about mere wishful dreaming. It's about expanding your perception of what's possible. Too often, people confine themselves to small ambitions because they fear failure, rejection, or the unknown. But the truth is, small thinking leads to small results. Those who achieve greatness do so because they push beyond the limits of what others consider realistic.

When you give yourself permission to dream big, you open the door to creativity, innovation, and boundless opportunities. You stop playing small and start looking at the world through the lens of possibility. Instead of asking, "Can I do this?" you begin to ask, "How can I make this happen?" That simple shift in mindset can change the entire trajectory of your life.

This chapter will challenge you to expand your vision, embrace boldness, and break free from limiting beliefs. We'll explore the psychology behind big goals, how they shape your mindset, and how to avoid the trap of settling for less than what you are truly capable of achieving.

By the end of this chapter, you will have a renewed sense of confidence in your ability to dream bigger than ever before—and the knowledge that thinking big is the first step to achieving big.

Why You Need a Dream That Excites You

A dream that excites you is more than just a goal—it's a compass that guides your actions, fuels your motivation, and keeps you moving forward even when obstacles arise. The difference between those who achieve extraordinary things and those who settle for less is often not talent, intelligence, or resources—it's their ability to connect with a dream that truly inspires them.

The Energy of an Exciting Dream

Have you ever noticed how much energy you have when you're doing something you're passionate about? Compare that to how drained you feel when working on something uninspiring. This is the difference between a dream that excites you and one that merely feels like an obligation. When your dream excites you, work stops feeling like work—it becomes a mission.

Exciting dreams provide a level of intrinsic motivation that external rewards cannot match. They generate enthusiasm, creativity, and resilience. When you're working toward something that genuinely inspires you, setbacks become easier to overcome because you're driven by something greater than short-term success.

The Science Behind Big Dreams

Psychologists have studied the impact of big, exciting goals on human behavior and have found that ambitious goals trigger higher levels of effort, creativity, and problem-solving. This is known as the Pygmalion effect, where higher expectations lead to greater performance. Simply put, when you aim higher, you push yourself beyond what you thought was possible.

Having an exciting dream also influences your dopamine levels—the brain's neurotransmitter responsible for motivation and reward. When you set and pursue a meaningful goal, dopamine is released, creating a sense of excitement and drive. This is why people who chase big, inspiring dreams often feel more alive and engaged in life.

How to Identify a Dream That Truly Excites You

Many people struggle to identify a dream that genuinely excites them. Here are some key ways to uncover what truly inspires you:

1. Listen to What Energizes You – Pay attention to the moments when you feel the most alive. What topics, activities, or ideas make you lose track of time? Your biggest dream often lies in those experiences.
2. Ignore the "Shoulds" – Society, family, and peers may have conditioned you to pursue what's "practical" or "safe." Strip away those external expectations and ask yourself: What do I want?

3. **Ask Yourself, "Would I Do This for Free?"** – If money were not a factor, what work or mission would you dedicate your life to? The answer often points to something that deeply excites you.
4. **Test Your Excitement** – If you think you've found your dream, talk about it. If you feel an energy surge and can't stop thinking about it, you're on the right track. If it feels dull or forced, keep exploring.
5. **Allow Yourself to Think Bigger** – If your dream doesn't scare you a little, it might not be big enough. Exciting dreams push you out of your comfort zone and force you to grow.

The Consequences of Settling for Less

Too many people settle for dreams that don't truly excite them. They choose careers, projects, or goals based on practicality rather than passion. While security and stability have their place, choosing a path that lacks excitement leads to boredom, disengagement, and regret.

When people suppress their true dreams in favor of what's "realistic," they often experience:

- Lack of motivation and enthusiasm
- Increased procrastination and avoidance
- A feeling of emptiness or unfulfillment
- Long-term regret for not pursuing what they truly wanted

Your Dream is Your Driving Force

When you identify and commit to a dream that excites you, you unlock a level of energy, creativity, and resilience that you never knew existed. You start waking up with purpose, feeling more engaged, and taking action that aligns with your ultimate vision.

Your dream is your unique gift to the world. The moment you allow yourself to embrace it fully, you stop merely existing and start truly living with purpose.

The Psychology of Big Goals

Setting big goals isn't just about ambition—it's about leveraging the science of human behavior to propel yourself toward greater success. Psychology plays a crucial role in how we perceive, approach, and ultimately achieve our goals. Understanding how big goals shape our mindset and behaviors will enable you to harness their power for extraordinary results.

The Neuroscience of Goal Setting

Our brains are wired to respond to challenges. When we set ambitious goals, we activate the brain's dopaminergic reward system, which is responsible for motivation and pleasure. Dopamine, often called the "feel-good neurotransmitter," spikes when we anticipate success. This means that simply having a bold vision triggers excitement, fuels perseverance, and sustains long-term commitment.

A study conducted by Harvard Business Review found that individuals with clearly defined and ambitious goals experienced heightened levels of cognitive focus and resilience. The more challenging the goal, the greater the brain's engagement in problem-solving and creative thinking.

The Growth Mindset and Big Goals

Dr. Carol Dweck, a renowned psychologist, introduced the concept of the growth mindset, which states that abilities and intelligence can be developed through effort and perseverance. People with a growth mindset embrace challenges, persist through setbacks, and view failure as an opportunity to learn.

Big goals cultivate a growth mindset because they require us to push beyond our comfort zone. When you set a goal that feels slightly beyond your current capabilities, your brain adapts by forming new neural connections. Over time, this strengthens your problem-solving abilities and increases your resilience.

Why Big Goals Increase Motivation

Motivation thrives on purpose. When we set small, uninspiring goals, our motivation levels fluctuate, leading to inconsistent progress. However, when we establish goals that feel meaningful and exciting, they create an intrinsic drive that keeps us engaged.

A famous study conducted by Edwin Locke and Gary Latham in the field of goal-setting theory found that specific, challenging goals lead to significantly higher performance than easy or vague goals. Big goals provide a clear sense of direction, making it easier to maintain focus and avoid distractions.

How Big Goals Change Your Behavior

When you set a big goal, you naturally shift your behavior to align with it. Your decisions, daily habits, and mindset begin to evolve in response to the demands of your goal. Here's how:

- Enhanced Focus – A bold goal acts as a guiding star, helping you prioritize what truly matters and eliminate distractions.
- Greater Resilience – When your goal is meaningful, you're more likely to push through setbacks and failures without losing momentum.
- Increased Creativity – Big goals require innovative thinking. They force you to explore new solutions and challenge traditional approaches.
- Higher Standards – The bigger the goal, the more you elevate your expectations for yourself, which leads to higher levels of personal and professional growth.

Overcoming Fear and Self-Doubt

One of the biggest obstacles to thinking big is fear of failure. Society often conditions us to seek security and avoid risks, but true success comes from embracing uncertainty. Those who achieve great things have learned to push past fear and take action despite doubts.

Here's how to overcome limiting beliefs and step into a mindset of limitless possibility:

1. Reframe failure as feedback – Every setback is an opportunity to refine your approach and grow stronger.
2. Visualize success daily – Neuroscientific research suggests that mental imagery enhances performance by training the brain to expect success.
3. Surround yourself with ambitious individuals – The people around you shape your beliefs. Engage with those who inspire and challenge you to aim higher.
4. Adopt a bias toward action – Rather than overanalyzing, commit to taking small, consistent steps toward your big goal.

Making Big Goals More Attainable

A common misconception is that big goals are overwhelming. In reality, breaking them down into structured steps makes them much more achievable. Consider this approach:

- Set a Visionary Goal – Define a goal that stretches you beyond your current limits.
- Reverse Engineer the Steps – Identify what needs to happen at each stage to reach the goal.
- Commit to Daily Progress – Focus on small, meaningful actions that build momentum.
- Measure and Adapt – Regularly assess progress and adjust your strategy as needed.

By understanding the psychology behind big goals, you can rewire your brain for success, increase motivation, and take control of your future. Thinking big isn't just about ambition—it's about tapping into the full potential of your mind and leveraging proven psychological principles to make extraordinary success your new standard.

Avoiding the Trap of Small Thinking

Small thinking is the silent killer of ambition. It keeps people confined to what feels comfortable and achievable, often preventing them from realizing their full potential. Those who think small limit their goals, settle for mediocrity, and never fully tap into their creative or intellectual capabilities.

One of the biggest dangers of small thinking is that it reinforces limitations rather than possibilities. When you tell yourself that a certain dream is "too big" or "unrealistic," you subconsciously shut down any effort to pursue it. Over time, these thoughts become ingrained beliefs that dictate the course of your life.

Small thinking also makes people more risk-averse, preferring comfort over challenge. This fear of failure keeps them from taking bold steps toward what they truly want. Instead, they settle for a life of playing it safe, never daring to break free from the ordinary.

How Small Thinking Manifests

Small thinking manifests in many ways, including:

- Fear of failure – The belief that taking risks will lead to embarrassment or loss.
- Settling for what's easy – Choosing paths that require minimal effort rather than striving for greatness.
- Lack of self-belief – Assuming you're not "good enough" to achieve something extraordinary.
- Listening to naysayers – Allowing negative influences to dictate what you think is possible.
- Procrastination – Avoiding big goals because they seem overwhelming.
- Rigid Comfort Zones – Clinging to familiarity even when it limits growth.
- Excuse-Driven Mindset – Using reasons like "I don't have enough time" or "I'm too old/young" as justification for not trying.
- Comparing Yourself to Others – Believing that success is reserved for people who are more talented, richer, or luckier than you.
- Not Taking Ownership – Thinking that external circumstances dictate success, rather than personal effort and choices.

Each of these behaviors stems from the same root problem: an unwillingness to push beyond one's current limits. If left unchecked, small thinking becomes a habit that shapes every aspect of your life.

The Cost of Thinking Small

When you allow small thinking to dictate your decisions, you pay a significant price:

- Missed opportunities – Big opportunities are often disguised as challenges. If you think small, you may never even consider them.
- Low self-worth – When you settle for less than you're capable of, you reinforce a belief that you're not worthy of more.
- Regret – The greatest regret people have later in life is not going after their biggest dreams.
- Lack of fulfillment – Small thinking keeps you in a cycle of comfort rather than growth, leaving you feeling unfulfilled.
- Diminished Creativity – Thinking small restricts problem-solving ability and limits innovation.
- Limited Influence – Those who think small don't inspire others to take bold actions, which limits their ability to make an impact.

Expanding Your Capacity for Big Thinking

To escape the trap of small thinking, you need to rewire your brain to embrace possibility, ambition, and growth. Here's how:

1. Expand Your Exposure – Surround yourself with people, books, and environments that challenge your thinking. The more you see examples of people achieving

incredible things, the more you realize that greatness is attainable.
2. Challenge Your Own Beliefs – Question any thought that tells you something is impossible. Ask yourself, "What if this *was* possible? What would I need to do to make it happen?"
3. Develop a Bias for Action – Instead of hesitating or waiting for the perfect moment, take immediate steps toward your big goals. Even small actions build momentum and dismantle limiting beliefs.
4. Embrace the Unknown – The most successful people in the world don't have all the answers when they start. They figure things out along the way. Train yourself to see uncertainty as an opportunity, not a barrier.
5. Redefine Failure – View setbacks as stepping stones, not stop signs. The greatest breakthroughs often come from learning experiences.
6. Adopt a '10X Thinking' Strategy – Set goals that are 10 times bigger than what you initially think is possible. The bigger the goal, the more creative and resourceful you become.
7. Surround Yourself with Big Thinkers – Engage with ambitious individuals who inspire you to push past perceived limitations.
8. Ask Better Questions – Instead of asking, "Can I do this?" ask, "How can I make this happen?"
9. Commit to Lifelong Learning – The more knowledge and skills you acquire, the bigger your perspective on what's possible.

10. Visualize Success Daily – Studies show that mentally rehearsing success increases your likelihood of achieving it.

Replacing Small Thinking with Abundance Thinking

Small thinking is rooted in scarcity—the idea that there's only so much success, money, or opportunity available. Those who think small operate from a place of limitation, believing that if someone else wins, they must lose.

Big thinkers, on the other hand, embrace an abundance mindset. They believe opportunities are infinite, success is available to everyone, and setbacks are temporary. This shift in perspective transforms how they approach challenges and unlocks a world of possibility.

How to Shift to an Abundance Mindset

- Practice Gratitude – Focus on what you already have rather than what you lack.
- Look for Opportunities, Not Obstacles – Instead of seeing problems, train yourself to find solutions.
- Celebrate the Success of Others – Instead of envying people who achieve greatness, use their success as proof that it's possible for you too.
- Focus on Growth, Not Scarcity – Understand that skills, knowledge, and opportunities expand the more you invest in them.

- Be Willing to Invest in Yourself – Whether it's time, education, or mentorship, those who think big invest in their own growth.

Chapter 2: Clarity Over Chaos

Ambition without clarity is like setting sail without a map. You may have a vision of where you want to go, but without precise direction, you will drift aimlessly, lost in the sea of possibilities, distractions, and uncertainty. Many people have dreams, but few take the time to define them with enough clarity to make achievement inevitable.

The truth is, success isn't just about working hard; it's about working on the right things with absolute focus. Clarity is what separates high-achievers from those who remain stuck in a cycle of wishful thinking. Without it, effort gets wasted on low-priority tasks, motivation dwindles, and procrastination takes over. But when your vision is crystal clear, every decision, action, and resource is directed toward meaningful progress.

This chapter is about bringing order to the chaos of ambition. We will explore how to define your vision with precision, introduce the Topify Vision Framework to help structure your goals, and show you how to turn vague ideas into actionable clarity. By the end of this chapter, you will know exactly where you're going and how to get there.

Clarity isn't just about knowing what you want—it's about removing distractions, eliminating doubt, and aligning your energy with your highest priorities. The world is full of opportunities, but without clear focus, these opportunities become overwhelming rather than empowering. Many people fail, not because they lack ability, but because they lack direction.

When you develop absolute clarity, you remove hesitation. Decisions become easier, distractions lose their power, and momentum builds effortlessly. Every step forward reinforces your confidence, creating a cycle of success that feels natural rather than forced. Clarity transforms effort into effectiveness, ensuring that your hard work moves you forward instead of keeping you busy without progress.

This is your moment to shift from scattered effort to focused execution. It's time to stop reacting and start creating with precision. Let's bring clarity to your ambition and make your vision a reality.

Defining Your Vision with Precision

Clarity is the foundation of achievement. Without a clear vision, you are at the mercy of external circumstances, constantly reacting rather than proactively shaping your future. Many people have vague aspirations—they want success, happiness, or financial freedom—but without specificity, these desires remain nothing more than wishful thinking.

To turn an idea into reality, you must define it with absolute precision. A vague vision leads to vague actions, while a precise vision sharpens focus and directs every effort toward meaningful progress. The clearer your vision, the greater your ability to make confident decisions and take purposeful action.

The Power of a Clear Vision

A well-defined vision acts as a compass. It provides direction, eliminates distractions, and ensures that every action aligns with your greater purpose. When you have clarity, decision-making becomes easier, motivation increases, and distractions lose their power over you.

People who lack vision often find themselves:

- Drifting from one opportunity to another without real progress
- Feeling overwhelmed by too many options
- Struggling with indecision and second-guessing
- Wasting time on activities that don't serve their long-term goals

A clear vision eliminates these challenges by setting a clear path forward. It helps you filter out distractions and prioritize what truly matters.

How to Define Your Vision with Precision

1. Be Specific – Instead of saying, "I want to be successful," define what success means to you. Is it financial independence? A thriving business? A balanced life? Get as specific as possible.
2. Create a Vision Statement – Write down your vision in a concise statement that captures the essence of what you want to achieve. This acts as a constant reminder of your goals.

3. Make It Measurable – A powerful vision is one that can be tracked. Include tangible milestones so you can measure progress.
4. Ensure It's Meaningful – Your vision should resonate deeply with you. If it doesn't inspire you, it won't sustain you through challenges.
5. Visualize It Daily – Spend time each day envisioning your success. This reinforces belief in your vision and strengthens your commitment to achieving it.
6. Align It with Your Core Values – Your vision should reflect what is most important to you. When your goals are aligned with your values, motivation and fulfillment follow.
7. Define the Why – Ask yourself why this vision matters to you. A strong purpose strengthens your resilience and commitment.

Breaking Down a Vision into Actionable Steps

Having a clear vision is only the beginning. The next step is translating it into daily actions. Here's how:

- Identify Key Milestones – Break your vision into major steps that signal progress.
- Set SMART Goals – Ensure your goals are Specific, Measurable, Achievable, Relevant, and Time-bound.
- Create a Strategic Plan – Outline the steps needed to reach each milestone.
- Develop Daily Habits – Align your routines with your vision.

- Track Progress – Regularly assess your progress and adjust as needed.

Overcoming Barriers to Clarity

Even with the best intentions, obstacles can cloud your vision. Here's how to overcome them:

- Fear of Failure – Fear often prevents people from defining bold visions. Accept that failure is part of growth.
- Too Many Choices – Narrow your focus by eliminating non-essential pursuits.
- External Influences – Avoid letting others dictate your vision. Stay true to what excites you.
- Lack of Confidence – Build confidence by taking small, consistent steps toward your vision.
- Overwhelm – Break your vision down into smaller, manageable steps.

The Science Behind a Strong Vision

Studies have shown that people with clearly defined visions experience higher motivation, increased persistence, and greater overall well-being. The human brain thrives on clarity—when you have a specific goal, your mind works to align thoughts and actions to achieve it.

Dr. Gail Matthews, a psychology professor, conducted a study on goal-setting and found that people who wrote down their goals were 42% more likely to achieve them than those who didn't. Writing your vision down makes it real and tangible, increasing commitment and accountability.

Real-Life Examples of Visionary Thinkers

Consider individuals who have changed the world—Elon Musk, Oprah Winfrey, and Steve Jobs. Each of them had an exceptionally clear vision of what they wanted to create. Their precision in defining their vision allowed them to persist through adversity, make bold decisions, and inspire millions.

- Elon Musk envisioned a world where humans could live on Mars. His unwavering clarity in that vision has fueled the rapid innovation of SpaceX.
- Oprah Winfrey built an empire based on her vision of empowering people through media.
- Steve Jobs had a crystal-clear vision for Apple—to create intuitive, beautifully designed technology that enhances lives.

Aligning Your Vision with Action

Defining your vision is only the first step; aligning your daily actions with your vision is what turns ideas into achievements. Break your vision down into actionable steps and create a strategy that ensures consistent progress.

Ask yourself daily:

- Are my actions today bringing me closer to my vision?

- What obstacles are preventing clarity and progress?
- How can I refine my approach to stay aligned with my vision?

Precision in vision leads to precision in execution. The clearer you are about where you're going, the faster and more effectively you will get there. Define your vision with precision, and watch as your path to success becomes unmistakably clear.

The Topify Vision Framework

Clarity is the key to transforming ambition into action, but most people struggle to define their vision in a structured way. This is where the Topify Vision Framework comes in—a step-by-step process designed to take your big ideas and transform them into a clear, actionable roadmap for success.

Many goal-setting systems focus on the end result but fail to provide a structured approach to getting there. The Topify Vision Framework bridges that gap, ensuring that your vision is not only ambitious but also practical, measurable, and deeply aligned with your personal and professional goals.

Why You Need a Framework for Your Vision

Most people fail to achieve their biggest dreams, not because they lack motivation, but because they lack clarity and structure. A vision that is too vague or overwhelming can lead to:

- Paralysis by analysis—overthinking without taking action

- Inconsistent focus—getting distracted by short-term goals that don't align with the bigger picture
- Lack of momentum—struggling to make progress because the path forward is unclear
- Loss of motivation—getting discouraged by uncertainty and obstacles

A well-defined framework eliminates these barriers by breaking down your vision into five core elements:

1. The Dream – What is the big idea that excites and inspires you?
2. The Why – Why does this vision matter to you?
3. The Strategy – How will you bring this vision to life?
4. The Action Plan – What steps will you take every day to move forward?
5. The Tracking System – How will you measure progress and stay accountable?

Each of these elements plays a critical role in transforming your vision into a clear, structured plan that leads to real results.

Step 1: The Dream – Defining Your Ultimate Vision

Every great achievement starts with a compelling dream. Your vision should be bold, inspiring, and deeply personal. It's not about what others expect from you—it's about what excites you the most.

Ask yourself:

- What do I want to create, achieve, or change in my life?
- If success was guaranteed, what would I pursue?
- What idea keeps me awake at night with excitement?
- How does this vision align with my core values?

Write down your dream in a single, powerful sentence. This becomes the guiding star for everything you do.

Step 2: The Why – Finding Your Emotional Connection

Your why is the fuel that keeps you going when challenges arise. Without a strong emotional connection to your vision, motivation fades.

To strengthen your why:

- Identify the personal meaning behind your vision.
- Consider how achieving it will impact your life and others around you.
- Imagine the long-term consequences of not pursuing your dream—does that thought bother you?

A strong why makes success non-negotiable. When obstacles appear, it reminds you why you started in the first place.

Step 3: The Strategy – Mapping the Journey

Once you have a clear vision and purpose, the next step is to create a strategic plan. This involves breaking your vision into phases:

1. Short-Term (0-3 months) – Immediate steps to start building momentum
2. Mid-Term (3-12 months) – Bigger milestones that show measurable progress
3. Long-Term (1-5 years) – The ultimate goal and how it evolves over time

Each phase should be tied to specific goals that align with your vision. This ensures that every action moves you closer to success.

Step 4: The Action Plan – Turning Strategy into Daily Execution

Many people get stuck in planning mode and never move to execution. The key to success is breaking down your strategy into daily and weekly actions that keep you moving forward.

A powerful action plan includes:

- Prioritized tasks that focus on high-impact activities
- Time-blocking strategies to protect time for important work
- Accountability systems like journaling, mentorship, or mastermind groups

Every day, ask yourself: *What is the single most important action I can take today that moves me toward my vision?* By consistently taking small, meaningful steps, you build unstoppable momentum.

Step 5: The Tracking System – Measuring Progress & Staying Aligned

A vision without tracking is like driving without a map—you may be moving, but you have no idea if you're on the right path. Measuring progress ensures you stay focused and adjust as needed.

Track your vision by:

- Setting measurable goals – Use key performance indicators (KPIs) to track growth.
- Weekly and monthly reviews – Reflect on what's working and what needs improvement.
- Accountability check-ins – Share progress with a mentor, coach, or accountability partner.
- Celebrating milestones – Recognizing progress fuels motivation and keeps momentum high.

Tracking transforms your vision from an abstract idea into a tangible reality.

Turning Vague Ideas into Actionable Clarity

Many people have incredible ideas, but without structure, those ideas remain just that—ideas. The difference between those who achieve greatness and those who remain stuck in the realm of potential is clarity. An idea without clarity is like a car without fuel—it has potential, but it won't take you anywhere.

Actionable clarity is the process of turning vague thoughts into structured plans that lead to measurable results. Clarity is what transforms wishful thinking into real-world achievement. When you know exactly what you want and how to get there, success becomes inevitable.

Why Vague Ideas Hold You Back

Many people get stuck in idea limbo, where they think about their goals constantly but never take meaningful action. This happens because:

- The goal is too broad – "I want to be successful" is not an actionable goal.
- They don't know where to start – The first step is unclear, leading to hesitation.
- They overthink the process – Instead of acting, they spend time analyzing and second-guessing.
- Fear of failure creeps in – Without a clear roadmap, uncertainty leads to inaction.

Without clarity, your brain defaults to inaction because it lacks direction. The mind thrives on certainty, so when a goal is vague, it becomes overwhelming.

The Process of Turning Ideas into Clarity

To turn vague ideas into an actionable plan, follow these steps:

1. Define the Core Idea with Precision

Many ideas start off as a fuzzy concept. The key is refining your idea into something clear and concrete.

Ask yourself:

- What is the core purpose of this idea?
- Who does this idea serve?
- What specific outcome do I want to achieve?

For example, instead of saying, "I want to start a business," refine it to: "I want to create a high-quality organic snack brand that caters to health-conscious consumers."

2. Break It Down into Specific Goals

Once your idea is clear, you need to create structured goals that turn it into reality. Use the SMART method:

- Specific – Define exactly what you want.
- Measurable – How will you track progress?
- Achievable – Can you realistically accomplish it?
- Relevant – Does it align with your larger vision?
- Time-bound – When will you achieve it?

For example, instead of saying, *"I want to grow my business,"* reframe it as: *"I will acquire 1,000 paying customers within six months through social media marketing and direct outreach."*

3. Create a Roadmap with Milestones

Big goals can be overwhelming, so break them into smaller milestones.

Example: If your goal is to write a book, your roadmap might look like this:

- Month 1: Research and outline chapters
- Month 2: Write the first draft
- Month 3: Revise and edit
- Month 4: Finalize and publish

Each milestone represents a manageable step that keeps you moving forward.

4. Develop Daily and Weekly Actions

Success doesn't come from big leaps; it comes from consistent action.

Once you have your milestones, break them down into daily and weekly tasks. For example:

- Daily: Write 500 words for my book
- Weekly: Reach out to five potential mentors for feedback
- Monthly: Complete one major section of my book

By focusing on daily execution, you remove overwhelm and make success inevitable.

5. Eliminate Distractions and Prioritize

Once you have a clear plan, you need to protect your focus.

- Identify time-wasters – Social media, TV, and unnecessary meetings drain time.
- Prioritize high-impact tasks – Work on the tasks that bring the greatest results.
- Use the 80/20 Rule – Focus 80% of your effort on the 20% of actions that drive the most impact.

Clarity isn't just about knowing what to do—it's about knowing what NOT to do.

6. Measure Progress and Adjust as Needed

Even with a great plan, adjustments are necessary. Regularly review your progress and ask:

- What's working well?
- What needs improvement?
- Where am I getting stuck?

By evaluating and adapting, you refine your strategy and stay on track.

Overcoming Common Clarity Killers

Even with the best planning, obstacles arise. Here's how to tackle them:

- Perfectionism – Don't wait for everything to be perfect before taking action. Start with what you have and refine along the way.
- Fear of failure – Failure is feedback. Every setback teaches you what to improve.
- Lack of motivation – Reconnect with your *why*. Remind yourself why this goal matters.
- Information overload – Don't get stuck researching forever. Set a deadline to make decisions and take action.

The Science Behind Clarity and Success

Studies have shown that clarity increases motivation and performance. Neuroscientific research suggests that when a goal is clear and specific, the brain engages the prefrontal cortex, which is responsible for decision-making and goal execution.

A study by Dr. Gail Matthews found that people who wrote down their goals were 42% more likely to achieve them than those who didn't. The act of writing clarifies thoughts, reinforces commitment, and turns an abstract idea into something real.

Summary of Part 1: The Dream

From Vision to Reality: Unlocking the Power of Big Dreams

Every great achievement starts with a dream—an audacious vision that ignites passion and fuels persistence. Part 1: The Dream explores the power of thinking big, the importance of clarity, and how to turn aspirations into structured plans that lead to real success.

The Power of Thinking Big

Thinking big is the foundation of extraordinary success. Most people limit their potential by thinking small, constrained by fear, self-doubt, or societal expectations. Big thinking expands possibilities, challenges perceived limitations, and creates opportunities that wouldn't exist otherwise.

A powerful dream must excite and inspire you. If your goal doesn't make you feel a deep sense of purpose, it's unlikely to sustain your motivation. Visionary leaders, game-changers, and pioneers all share one thing in common: a bold vision that pushes them beyond their comfort zone.

However, dreaming big isn't just about wishful thinking. It requires a shift in mindset—from focusing on obstacles to seeking solutions. To unlock your full potential, you must break free from small thinking and develop the courage to pursue ambitions that stretch you beyond your current capabilities.

The Psychology of Big Goals

Big goals have a profound psychological impact. They activate the brain's dopaminergic reward system, increasing motivation, focus, and resilience. When you set an ambitious target, your mind naturally starts working on ways to achieve it.

However, most people struggle with big goals because of fear—fear of failure, judgment, or inadequacy. Overcoming these fears requires a shift in perspective: failure isn't a stop sign; it's a stepping stone to success. Every major breakthrough in history was preceded by countless setbacks, and the ability to push through them defines true achievers.

Avoiding the Trap of Small Thinking

Small thinking is a dangerous trap that leads to stagnation. It manifests in many forms: procrastination, playing it safe, listening to naysayers, or settling for mediocrity. People who think small avoid risks, but in doing so, they also avoid opportunities.

To escape this mindset, you must:

- Challenge limiting beliefs – Question assumptions about what's possible.
- Expand your environment – Surround yourself with ambitious, driven individuals.
- Take decisive action – Progress comes from consistent, focused effort.

- Embrace uncertainty – The most successful people are comfortable with ambiguity and adapt as they go.

Turning Dreams into Clarity

A dream without clarity remains a fantasy. This is why defining your vision with precision is crucial. A vague goal leads to vague results. Successful individuals turn ideas into structured plans by outlining specific objectives, creating milestones, and setting measurable targets.

Clarity eliminates distractions and provides a clear roadmap. It allows you to filter out unnecessary noise and focus on high-impact actions. The more defined your vision, the easier it becomes to align your daily actions with your ultimate goal.

Part 2: The Strategy

A powerful vision is only as strong as the strategy that turns it into reality. Dreams without action remain fantasies, but when backed by a clear, structured plan, they become inevitable. Part 2 of this book is about bridging the gap between ambition and execution—transforming your vision into an achievable roadmap.

Most people fail to reach their goals, not because they lack motivation, but because they lack a system that keeps them moving forward. They overcomplicate the process, get overwhelmed, or fail to track progress effectively. Success isn't just about setting a goal—it's about creating a framework that allows you to make consistent progress every single day.

This section introduces the Topify Method's strategic approach to goal achievement. Instead of relying on willpower or motivation alone, you will learn how to reverse engineer success, prioritize effectively, and build habits that drive long-term results.

In Chapter 3: Reverse Engineering Success, we break big goals into actionable steps, ensuring that you always know what to do next. The 90-day sprint approach provides a structured way to maintain momentum, while designing a system tailored to your strengths ensures that you stay consistent.

In Chapter 4: The Topify Quadrants, we introduce a simple but powerful method for prioritization. You'll learn how to categorize your tasks into Essential, Growth, Delegation, and

Elimination quadrants—allowing you to cut distractions, eliminate busy work, and focus on what truly moves the needle.

Finally, in Chapter 5: The Science of Habit Stacking, we explore how to build routines that support your goals. You'll discover how small, daily actions compound over time to create exponential results. By mastering the habit-stacking method, you'll ensure that success becomes automatic rather than something you have to chase.

By the end of this section, you will have a step-by-step strategy for turning your vision into a structured, repeatable process. No more vague plans or inconsistent effort—just a clear, actionable system that ensures you are always moving forward.

It's time to stop hoping for success and start engineering it. Let's dive in.

Chapter 3: Reverse Engineering Success

Success isn't an accident—it's the result of deliberate action, strategic planning, and consistent execution. Yet, most people set goals without a clear roadmap to achieve them. They focus on where they want to go but fail to define the exact steps that will take them there. This is where reverse engineering success becomes a game-changer.

Instead of setting a lofty goal and hoping to figure it out along the way, reverse engineering works by starting at the end—your ultimate goal—and breaking it down into structured, actionable steps. By working backward, you eliminate guesswork and create a direct path to achievement.

Think of any major accomplishment: building a business, writing a book, completing a marathon. Every one of these achievements starts with the outcome in mind, followed by a well-structured plan to make it happen. Successful people don't leave their progress to chance; they break down big goals into manageable milestones that ensure continuous momentum.

In this chapter, you'll learn how to deconstruct big goals into actionable steps, ensuring that you always know what to do next. We'll introduce the 90-day sprint approach, a powerful system that focuses on short-term execution for long-term success. You'll also discover how to design a system that works for your unique strengths, lifestyle, and ambitions.

By the end of this chapter, you will no longer feel overwhelmed by big aspirations. Instead, you will have a clear, strategic process that makes even the most ambitious goals feel achievable. Success isn't about working harder—it's about working smarter with a plan that ensures progress every step of the way.

It's time to take control of your goals and reverse-engineer your path to success. Let's get started.

Breaking Big Goals into Actionable Steps

Why Big Goals Often Fail

Setting big goals is easy—achieving them is where most people struggle. The reason? Big goals can feel overwhelming. They seem too distant, too difficult, or too abstract to take immediate action. When faced with a massive objective, many people freeze, procrastinate, or burn out before making significant progress.

The solution? Breaking goals into structured, actionable steps. When you deconstruct a big goal into smaller, achievable milestones, you eliminate uncertainty and create momentum. Instead of feeling stuck at the starting line, you gain clarity on what needs to happen next. Success isn't about giant leaps—it's about consistent, small steps in the right direction.

Step 1: Define Your Ultimate Goal with Clarity

Before breaking a goal into steps, you need to define it with absolute precision. A vague goal leads to vague actions. Ask yourself:

- What does success look like?
- How will I measure achievement?
- What specific outcome am I aiming for?

For example, instead of saying, *"I want to get in shape,"* reframe it as *"I will lose 15 pounds and run a 5K within four months."* The clearer your goal, the easier it becomes to break it into tangible steps.

Step 2: Work Backward – Reverse Engineering the Goal

One of the most effective strategies for turning a big goal into manageable steps is reverse engineering. Instead of figuring out where to start, work from the end result backward to determine what needs to happen at each stage.

For example, if your goal is to launch a successful online business in one year, break it down like this:

1. Final goal: Generate $10,000/month in revenue.
2. 6-month milestone: Have a fully built website and marketing system in place.
3. 3-month milestone: Develop a core product/service and validate market demand.
4. 1-month milestone: Research niche, build audience, and set up initial branding.
5. Weekly/daily actions: Create content, reach out to potential customers, refine strategy.

By breaking your goal into phases, you create a step-by-step roadmap that eliminates guesswork and provides a clear action plan.

Step 3: Identify Key Milestones

Milestones act as checkpoints on your journey toward a goal. They help you stay motivated and ensure that you're on track. Instead of focusing solely on the final result, milestones break the journey into bite-sized victories that build confidence.

For example, if your goal is to write a book in six months:

- Milestone 1: Complete outline (2 weeks)
- Milestone 2: Write the first 10,000 words (1 month)
- Milestone 3: Reach 40,000 words (3 months)
- Milestone 4: First draft complete (5 months)
- Milestone 5: Final edit and submission (6 months)

By hitting these milestones, the overwhelming idea of "writing a book" becomes a series of manageable targets.

Step 4: Break Each Milestone into Daily & Weekly Tasks

Once you have milestones, break them down further into weekly and daily tasks. This ensures that you make consistent progress and avoid last-minute stress.

For example, if your next milestone is to write 10,000 words in a month, break it down like this:

- Weekly goal: Write 2,500 words.

- Daily goal: Write 500 words per day.

With this structure, progress becomes automatic. Instead of wondering, *"What should I do today?"* you already have a clear plan of action.

Step 5: Create a System for Tracking Progress

Having a plan is one thing—staying accountable is another. A tracking system helps measure progress and ensures that you're consistently moving forward.

Here are a few ways to track your progress:

- Journaling: Write down daily accomplishments and obstacles.
- Task Lists: Use a digital or physical checklist to track completed tasks.
- Progress Charts: Visually monitor milestones using a spreadsheet or planner.
- Accountability Partners: Share your goals with someone who will hold you accountable.

By tracking results, you create motivation and a sense of momentum, which keeps you committed to long-term success.

Step 6: Adjust and Adapt as Needed

No plan is perfect. Challenges, unexpected obstacles, and changing circumstances will always arise. Instead of getting discouraged, treat setbacks as opportunities to refine your approach.

Regularly ask yourself:

- What's working well?
- What's holding me back?
- What adjustments need to be made?

Flexibility ensures that even if you miss a milestone, you can adapt and get back on track without abandoning the entire goal.

Step 7: Celebrate Progress Along the Way

Finally, acknowledge and reward progress. Celebrating small wins keeps motivation high and reinforces positive habits. Whether it's finishing a draft, hitting a fitness milestone, or landing a first client, take time to appreciate your growth.

Ways to celebrate include:

- Taking a break or rewarding yourself with something enjoyable.
- Reflecting on how far you've come.
- Sharing successes with supportive friends or mentors.

The 90-Day Sprint Approach

Why Traditional Goal Setting Fails

Most people set goals with the best intentions, yet they fail to maintain momentum. Long-term goals, especially those set for a year or more, often lose urgency. A year feels like a long time, which leads to procrastination, distractions, and a lack of immediate accountability.

The solution? A 90-day sprint approach.

Instead of setting distant goals with vague timelines, the 90-day sprint focuses on achieving clear, measurable outcomes in just three months. This short-term approach forces action, maintains motivation, and allows for quick adjustments along the way. It transforms goals from distant aspirations into urgent priorities.

What is the 90-Day Sprint Approach?

A 90-day sprint is a high-intensity, focused execution period where you commit to achieving a specific goal within three months. It is long enough to create meaningful progress but short enough to maintain urgency and motivation.

Unlike traditional goal-setting, which often lacks structure, the 90-day sprint follows a clear system:

1. Define one major outcome – A specific, measurable result you want to achieve in 90 days.

2. Break it down into milestones – Key checkpoints to hit along the way.
3. Prioritize weekly and daily actions – Focus on high-impact activities that directly contribute to success.
4. Track progress aggressively – Review achievements weekly and adjust if needed.
5. Reflect, recalibrate, and repeat – After 90 days, evaluate, learn, and set a new sprint.

By compressing a goal into a high-intensity period, the 90-day sprint eliminates procrastination and creates a sense of urgency that drives rapid progress.

Step 1: Defining Your 90-Day Goal

Your sprint must begin with absolute clarity. Instead of setting multiple competing priorities, pick ONE big goal that will have the most impact on your life or business.

Ask yourself:

- What is the most important thing I need to accomplish in the next 90 days?
- What outcome would create significant momentum toward my larger vision?
- How will I measure success at the end of 90 days?

Your goal must be specific, measurable, and meaningful.

Examples of Strong 90-Day Goals:

- Launch and sell 100 units of a new product.
- Lose 10 pounds and build a consistent workout habit.
- Write 30,000 words of a book manuscript.
- Acquire 10 new high-value clients.

Once defined, your goal becomes your central focus for the next 90 days—no distractions, no excuses.

Step 2: Breaking It Down Into Milestones

To ensure consistent progress, divide your 90-day goal into three monthly milestones.

For example, if your goal is to write 30,000 words for a book:

- Month 1: Write 10,000 words, establish daily writing habit.
- Month 2: Reach 20,000 words, refine structure, edit sections.
- Month 3: Complete 30,000 words, begin final revisions.

Milestones provide a clear roadmap and prevent last-minute scrambling to meet deadlines.

Step 3: Planning Weekly & Daily Actions

Now that you have milestones, break them down further into weekly and daily actions.

Each week, determine 3-5 key tasks that move you toward your goal. Each day, identify the one most important task (MIT) that directly contributes to your sprint's success.

Using the book-writing example:

- Week 1: Outline key chapters, write 2,500 words.
- Daily MIT: Write 500 words before 10 AM.

This method ensures that every single day contributes to meaningful progress.

Step 4: Tracking Progress and Staying Accountable

What gets measured gets managed. Tracking your progress keeps you accountable and helps you stay on course.

Ways to track your sprint:

- Daily progress logs – Write down key achievements each day.
- Weekly reflections – Assess what worked, what didn't, and what needs adjustment.
- Accountability partners – Share your goals with someone who will keep you on track.
- Scorecards or habit trackers – Visually track progress using spreadsheets or apps.

The key is real-time feedback—adjust your plan as needed to ensure continued success.

Step 5: Reflecting and Recalibrating

At the end of 90 days, take time to reflect on your sprint:

- What did you accomplish?
- What challenges did you overcome?
- What strategies worked best?
- What would you do differently next time?

Use these insights to refine your approach for the next sprint.

Why the 90-Day Sprint Works

1. Creates Urgency – With a short timeline, you eliminate excuses and act with intensity.
2. Forces Prioritization – Instead of juggling endless goals, you focus on what truly matters.
3. Builds Momentum – Achieving meaningful results in 90 days fuels motivation for the next sprint.
4. Encourages Flexibility – Short cycles allow for quick adjustments and continuous improvement.
5. Delivers Tangible Results – Unlike vague year-long resolutions, the sprint approach guarantees real progress.

Designing a System That Works for You

The Power of a Personalized System

Success isn't about working harder—it's about working smarter with a system tailored to your strengths, lifestyle, and goals. Many people struggle with consistency because they try to follow rigid, one-size-fits-all strategies that don't align with how they naturally operate. The key to sustainable achievement is designing a system that works for you, not against you.

A well-designed system eliminates decision fatigue, maximizes efficiency, and turns actions into habits. Instead of relying on motivation—which fluctuates—your system ensures progress happens automatically.

Why Most Productivity Systems Fail

Many traditional productivity systems fail because:

- They are too rigid – What works for someone else may not work for you.
- They rely on willpower – Willpower is unreliable; systems should function automatically.
- They lack adaptability – Life is unpredictable, and your system should adjust accordingly.
- They don't prioritize sustainability – A good system should fit your lifestyle, not disrupt it.

The solution? Create a flexible, personalized system that enhances your strengths and removes obstacles.

Step 1: Identify Your Strengths & Weaknesses

Before designing your system, assess how you naturally work best.

Ask yourself:

- Do I work better in the morning or evening?
- Am I most productive in short bursts or long sessions?
- What habits have helped me succeed in the past?
- What distractions frequently derail my progress?
- How do I respond to structure vs. flexibility?

Understanding these factors allows you to create a system aligned with your energy levels and work preferences.

Step 2: Define Your Core Priorities

Your system should focus on what truly matters. Define your non-negotiables by asking:

- What are the 3-5 most important things I need to focus on daily/weekly?
- What tasks generate the most meaningful progress toward my goals?
- What activities waste my time and energy?

Prioritizing these elements ensures your system is built around high-impact activities rather than busy work.

Step 3: Choose a Framework That Fits

Different people thrive under different systems. Here are a few effective models:

1. Time-Blocking Method

- Best for: People who need structure and focus
- How it works: Allocate specific time blocks to specific activities each day (e.g., 9-11 AM for deep work, 3-4 PM for admin tasks).
- Benefit: Reduces distractions and ensures important work gets done.

2. Thematic Workdays

- Best for: People juggling multiple projects or roles
- How it works: Assign specific days to specific tasks (e.g., Monday for strategy, Tuesday for meetings, Wednesday for content creation).
- Benefit: Helps maintain focus without constant task-switching.

3. The 90-Minute Work Cycle

- Best for: People who thrive in deep-focus sessions
- How it works: Work in 90-minute sprints followed by short breaks.

- Benefit: Aligns with natural energy rhythms and prevents burnout.

4. The Daily MIT (Most Important Task) Method
    - Best for: People who need a simple, flexible approach
    - How it works: Identify 1-3 top-priority tasks each day and complete them first.
    - Benefit: Ensures that progress is made on key goals even in unpredictable schedules.

Pick a system—or a combination—that aligns with how you naturally operate.

Step 4: Automate & Streamline Repetitive Tasks

Repetitive tasks drain mental energy. Automating and streamlining them frees up time for high-value activities.

Ways to streamline:

- Use scheduling tools – Automate meetings and reminders.
- Create templates – For emails, reports, and frequently used documents.
- Set recurring tasks – Automate bill payments, project check-ins, and recurring responsibilities.
- Outsource low-value tasks – Delegate tasks that don't require your expertise.

By removing friction, you allow your system to run smoothly without constant manual effort.

Step 5: Build Accountability & Feedback Loops

A great system keeps you accountable. Without accountability, even the best plans fall apart.

Ways to integrate accountability:

- Daily check-ins – Spend 5 minutes reviewing priorities each morning.
- Weekly reflections – Assess what worked, what didn't, and adjust accordingly.
- Accountability partners – Share progress with a friend, mentor, or mastermind group.
- Track your habits – Use a journal, planner, or app to monitor progress.

By regularly reviewing and refining your system, you ensure continuous improvement.

Step 6: Adapt & Evolve as Needed

Your system should evolve with you. Life circumstances, energy levels, and priorities change, so your approach should be flexible.

Questions to ask when adjusting:

- What's working well?
- Where am I struggling?

- What adjustments will improve consistency and efficiency?

A rigid system is destined to break. A flexible, evolving system adapts to keep you moving forward.

Chapter 4: The Topify Quadrants

One of the biggest challenges in achieving success isn't a lack of effort—it's misplaced effort. Most people work hard but struggle to make significant progress because they focus on the wrong tasks. They spend too much time on low-value activities, get distracted by urgent but unimportant tasks, or fail to delegate responsibilities that slow them down. The real key to high performance isn't just working harder—it's working on the right things.

That's where the Topify Quadrants come in. This framework provides a clear, structured method for prioritization, ensuring that your daily actions align with your long-term vision. By categorizing tasks into four essential areas—Essential, Growth, Delegation, and Elimination—you can cut through the noise, focus on what truly matters, and eliminate what doesn't.

The problem with traditional productivity methods is that they often treat all tasks as equally important. But not all actions have the same impact. Some tasks move you closer to success at an accelerated rate, while others drain energy and yield little return. The Topify Quadrants help you filter tasks based on their value, impact, and necessity.

In this chapter, you'll learn how to:

- Categorize tasks effectively using the four quadrants
- Prioritize high-impact activities that lead to real progress
- Delegate or eliminate tasks that waste time and slow you down

- Develop a decision-making framework to streamline your workflow

By the end of this chapter, you'll have a simple but powerful system to prioritize with confidence. You'll no longer feel overwhelmed by endless to-do lists or distracted by tasks that don't truly matter. Instead, you'll work with precision and clarity, focusing only on the actions that drive results.

Let's dive in and take control of your time, energy, and productivity by mastering the Topify Quadrants.

The Four Types of Action: Essential, Growth, Delegation, Elimination

The Power of Prioritization

Success isn't just about doing more—it's about doing the right things. Many people waste time on tasks that don't move them forward, leading to frustration and burnout. The Topify Quadrants framework simplifies decision-making by categorizing every action into one of four key areas: Essential, Growth, Delegation, and Elimination.

This method ensures that you are always focused on high-impact tasks while reducing distractions and inefficiencies. By mastering these quadrants, you gain clarity, work smarter, and accelerate progress toward your goals.

Quadrant 1: Essential Actions – The Foundation of Progress

What It Includes: Essential actions are the core tasks that directly contribute to your most important goals. These are the non-negotiables—the actions that, if executed consistently, will generate meaningful results.

Examples:

- Delivering client work
- Creating revenue-generating activities
- Training and self-improvement in key skill areas
- Completing milestone projects directly tied to long-term success

Why It Matters: Many people spend too much time on urgent tasks but not enough on essential ones. By prioritizing essential actions, you ensure that your time is dedicated to high-value work that makes an impact.

How to Implement:

1. Identify your top three essential tasks each day.
2. Time-block these activities to ensure focus.
3. Measure success based on completion of these tasks rather than busyness.

Quadrant 2: Growth Actions – Investing in Future Success

What It Includes: Growth actions are the activities that don't provide immediate returns but are crucial for long-term success. These tasks expand your capabilities, build new opportunities, and improve efficiency.

Examples:

- Networking and building key relationships
- Learning new skills or certifications
- Research and strategic planning
- Improving systems and automation

Why It Matters: Growth actions set you up for bigger opportunities. While they may not feel urgent, they are essential for long-term sustainability and business scalability.

How to Implement:

1. Dedicate at least 20% of your week to growth actions.
2. Set clear learning or networking goals each month.
3. Treat personal and professional development as a priority, not an afterthought.

Quadrant 3: Delegation Actions – Freeing Your Time for Higher-Value Work

What It Includes: Delegation tasks are important but do not require your direct involvement. These should be handled by others to free up your time for essential and growth actions.

Examples:

- Administrative work (emails, scheduling, invoicing)
- Customer service and support
- Content repurposing and social media management
- Routine operational tasks

Why It Matters: Many high-performers struggle with delegation because they believe they must do everything themselves. However, scalability is impossible without handing off lower-priority tasks.

How to Implement:

1. Identify tasks that do not require your unique expertise.
2. Hire, outsource, or automate repetitive processes.
3. Focus your time on work that aligns with your strengths and goals.

Quadrant 4: Elimination Actions – Cutting Out What Holds You Back

What It Includes: Elimination tasks are the time-wasters, distractions, and low-value activities that do not contribute to your goals. These must be removed to create space for essential and growth actions.

Examples:

- Excessive social media scrolling
- Unproductive meetings

- Saying yes to obligations that don't align with your goals
- Tasks that feel "busy" but accomplish little

Why It Matters: Every minute spent on non-essential tasks is time taken away from what truly matters. Eliminating unnecessary tasks is just as powerful as adding productive ones.

How to Implement:

1. Conduct a weekly audit of where your time is going.
2. Identify 2-3 recurring tasks that don't add value and cut them.
3. Set clear boundaries to avoid distractions and unnecessary commitments.

Implementing the Four Quadrants into Your Daily Routine

Now that you understand the four types of action, it's time to integrate them into your workflow. Here's how:

1. Categorize Your Tasks – Each week, list all tasks and place them into one of the quadrants.
2. Prioritize Accordingly:
   - Essential: Schedule these first in your daily plan.
   - Growth: Allocate dedicated time each week.
   - Delegation: Hand these off to free up time.
   - Elimination: Remove or automate.
1. Review & Adjust Weekly: Continuously refine what's working and eliminate what isn't.

By consistently applying these quadrants, you cut through the noise, focus on impact, and streamline success. Mastering prioritization is the difference between working endlessly and working effectively. It's time to take control and focus only on what truly moves you forward.Prioritization Made Simple

The Simplicity of Prioritization: Choosing What Truly Matters

Most people think they're prioritizing their time wisely, but in reality, they're choosing tasks based on ease and instant gratification rather than true importance. We naturally gravitate toward the tasks that are urgent, feel productive, or provide a quick sense of accomplishment, but those aren't always the tasks that truly move us forward.

The key to achieving more isn't about doing more—it's about doing what truly matters, first and consistently. Prioritization shouldn't be complicated. In fact, it should be the simplest part of your day. The challenge is in shifting our mindset to focus on long-term progress over short-term rewards.

The Topify Method simplifies prioritization into one core principle: Identify your Top 5 Priorities and commit to completing your Top 1 Priority every day. This ensures that you focus on the most impactful actions, not just the ones that are easiest to check off.

The Trap of Prioritizing the Easy Over the Important

The biggest mistake people make is mistaking activity for productivity.

It's easy to:

- Respond to emails instead of working on a business strategy
- Organize your desk instead of making a sales call
- Read about exercise routines instead of actually exercising

Why? Because these tasks feel productive but come with little friction or discomfort. The real priorities—the ones that create breakthroughs—often require effort, risk, or deep focus.

The Topify Method helps overcome this tendency by forcing clarity: What is the single most important thing I can do today to make the biggest impact?

Step 1: Identify Your Top 5 Priorities

Each morning, take a moment to define the five most important tasks that will drive you closer to your goals. These are not just random to-dos—they are the highest-value actions that, if completed, will create real momentum.

Your Top 5 Priorities should:

- Directly contribute to long-term success
- Have measurable impact

- Push you outside your comfort zone

For example: "Write the first draft of my pitch deck" (High impact) "Watch an inspirational TED Talk" (Feels productive, but isn't progress)

By narrowing your focus to just five key actions, you eliminate unnecessary distractions and ensure that everything you do moves you forward.

Step 2: The Power of the Top 1 Priority

Your Top 1 Priority is the task that will make the biggest difference in your day. It's the action that, if completed, would bring you the most progress, relief, or momentum.

Why this works:

- It forces you to do what actually matters first
- It eliminates decision fatigue and wasted energy
- It builds confidence by creating daily wins

Ask yourself: *If I could only complete ONE thing today, what would have the biggest impact?*

Once identified, dedicate deep focus time to completing it before moving on to anything else.

Step 3: Work Through the Remaining Priorities in Order

After completing your Top 1 Priority, move through the rest of your Top 5 in order of importance. Some tasks will be completed quickly, while others may require more effort. The key is to ensure that each task meaningfully contributes to your long-term goals.

If a task remains unfinished by the end of the day, it rolls over to the next day—but only if it is still relevant and necessary.

Step 4: Simplify by Eliminating, Automating, or Delegating

A simple prioritization system isn't just about choosing the right tasks—it's about removing the wrong ones.

Ask yourself:

- Does this task actually matter, or am I just doing it because it's easy?
- Can this be automated or handled by someone else?
- Is this necessary, or am I doing it out of habit?

By eliminating distractions, automating repetitive tasks, and delegating low-value work, you create more space for deep, meaningful progress.

Step 5: Review & Reset Daily

At the end of each day, reflect on:

- Did I complete my Top 1 Priority?
- Did I fall into the trap of prioritizing the easy over the important?
- How can I refine my focus for tomorrow?

Then, reset your Top 5 Priorities for the next day. This simple habit ensures constant alignment with your biggest goals.

How to Cut the Noise and Focus on Impact

The Challenge of Modern Distractions

The modern world is designed to pull your attention in a thousand directions. Between endless notifications, emails, social media, and meetings, it's easy to feel overwhelmed. We often mistake being busy for being productive, but real progress comes from cutting the noise and focusing on what truly moves the needle.

If you want to achieve meaningful results, you must be deliberate about eliminating distractions and channeling your energy into high-impact work. This isn't about doing more—it's about ensuring that what you do truly matters.

Why We Struggle to Focus on High-Impact Work

Most people aren't unproductive because they lack effort; they're unproductive because they spend too much time on low-value tasks. Here's why this happens:

1. We Confuse Urgency with Importance – Many tasks feel urgent (emails, requests, notifications), but they don't contribute to long-term success.
2. We Gravitate Toward Easy Wins – Checking notifications and responding to messages provides a false sense of progress, but it doesn't move us forward.

3. **We Overcommit to Non-Essential Tasks** – Saying yes too often leaves us with no time for deep, meaningful work.
4. **We Lack Clear Boundaries** – Without structure, distractions take over our most productive hours.
5. **We Haven't Built a Focus System** – Without a framework for prioritization, we react to whatever grabs our attention first.

Recognizing these tendencies is the first step to regaining control over your focus and maximizing impact.

Step 1: Define What Truly Matters

To cut the noise, you must define your high-impact tasks. These are the small number of critical actions that generate the majority of your results.

Ask yourself:

- What are the top 5% of tasks that create the biggest impact on my goals?
- What work, if eliminated, would have little to no real consequences?
- If I could only complete one task today, which one would make the biggest difference?

By defining your priorities upfront, you ensure that everything else becomes noise.

Step 2: Set Rules to Filter Out Distractions

To eliminate distractions, establish clear decision-making rules about what deserves your time and attention.

Use these filters:

- The One Task Test – If I could only complete one thing today, what would have the biggest impact?
- The 80/20 Rule – Does this task fall within the top 20% of activities that create 80% of my results?
- The Elimination Test – If I removed this task from my schedule, would it actually matter?

By applying these principles, you say no to non-essential work and free up time for what matters most.

Step 3: Reduce Input Overload

The more information you consume, the more fragmented your focus becomes. Be intentional about what you allow into your mind.

Ways to reduce input overload:

- Limit time spent on email & social media – Check messages at set times instead of constantly reacting.
- Unsubscribe from distractions – Remove yourself from unnecessary email lists and notifications.
- Be selective with content consumption – Avoid mindless scrolling and only consume information that supports your goals.

By controlling input, you create mental space for deep, focused work.

Step 4: Optimize Your Work Environment

Your environment plays a critical role in your ability to focus. Design a workspace that minimizes distractions and supports high-impact work.

Key adjustments:

- Turn off non-essential notifications – Let email and messages wait until designated times.
- Use time-blocking techniques – Schedule deep work sessions with zero interruptions.
- Keep your workspace clean and organized – A clutter-free space helps maintain mental clarity.
- Use techniques that enhance focus – Create an environment that signals your brain it's time to work.

By intentionally shaping your environment, you make focus effortless.

Step 5: Build Deep Work Rituals

To cut through the noise, create rituals that reinforce uninterrupted deep work.

- Start your day with your most important task – Don't check messages before making progress on a high-priority project.

- Use the 90-minute sprint method – Work in deep-focus sessions, then take short breaks.
- Batch similar tasks together – Handle emails, meetings, and admin work in dedicated blocks of time.
- Adopt a "no unnecessary meetings" rule – Protect valuable focus hours.

When deep work becomes a habit, distractions lose their grip on you.

Step 6: Audit & Eliminate Low-Value Activities

Every week, review where your time is going. Track your tasks and identify distractions that are consuming energy without producing meaningful results.

Ask yourself:

- What tasks felt urgent but were ultimately unimportant?
- Where did I waste the most time?
- What low-value tasks can I eliminate, automate, or delegate?

The goal is to continuously refine your focus, ensuring more of your time is spent on high-impact work.

Step 7: Make Focus a Daily Habit

Long-term impact comes from consistently choosing deep work over distractions.

- Start small – Focus on eliminating just one major distraction this week.
- Be patient – Focus is a skill that strengthens over time.
- Celebrate wins – Each distraction eliminated is progress toward mastering focus.

By treating focus as a daily discipline, you ensure that noise never dictates your work again.

Chapter 5: The Science of Habit Stacking

Success isn't built on one-time bursts of effort—it's built on consistent daily actions that compound over time. The difference between those who achieve extraordinary results and those who remain stuck isn't just motivation; it's the habits they embed into their lives.

But building new habits can feel overwhelming. Most people try to overhaul their routines overnight, only to lose momentum and fall back into old patterns. This is where habit stacking comes in—a simple yet powerful strategy that makes it easy to integrate new behaviors into your daily life by attaching them to habits you already do.

Rather than relying on willpower, habit stacking creates a seamless way to build productive behaviors without disrupting your existing routine. It leverages the brain's natural tendency to follow familiar patterns, making it easier to adopt new habits with minimal effort.

In this chapter, we'll break down the science behind habit stacking and how you can use it to:

- Develop non-negotiable daily routines that support your goals
- Leverage momentum by linking new habits to existing ones
- Use the compound effect to create exponential growth over time

By the end of this chapter, you'll have a clear, repeatable system for building habits that stick—ensuring that progress becomes automatic rather than something you have to constantly force.

Let's dive into the power of habit stacking and how it can transform the way you approach achievement.

Building Non-Negotiable Daily Routines

The Power of Daily Routines

Success is not determined by what you do occasionally but by what you do consistently. Your habits shape your results, and your results shape your life. The world's highest achievers—from elite athletes to top CEOs—don't leave their progress to chance. Instead, they rely on non-negotiable daily routines that keep them on track, no matter what.

A non-negotiable daily routine is a set of habits that are so deeply ingrained into your day that skipping them is not an option. These habits create momentum, reduce decision fatigue, and allow you to operate at peak performance.

Why Non-Negotiable Routines Work

The human brain thrives on routine. When you establish clear, consistent habits, you free up mental energy for more important decisions. Daily routines work because:

- They eliminate guesswork and decision fatigue.
- They reinforce discipline and consistency.

- They create a foundation for long-term success.
- They prevent procrastination by establishing structure.
- They help you develop the identity of someone who follows through.

The key to success isn't just about setting goals—it's about building the daily systems that make achieving those goals inevitable.

Step 1: Identify Your High-Impact Habits

To create a non-negotiable routine, you must first identify the habits that will have the greatest impact on your success. Not all habits are created equal—some will move you forward faster than others.

Ask yourself:

- What daily actions will bring me closer to my biggest goals?
- What small, consistent efforts will compound over time?
- What habits do the people I admire practice daily?

Some of the most effective high-impact habits include:

- Morning Movement: Exercising or stretching to activate your body and mind.
- Focused Deep Work: Allocating uninterrupted time for your most important task.
- Journaling or Planning: Reviewing your progress and setting daily intentions.

- Mindfulness or Meditation: Practicing focus and stress management.
- Reading or Learning: Investing in continuous growth and knowledge.

Step 2: Start Small and Build Momentum

Many people fail to build daily routines because they try to change too much at once. The key is to start small and build momentum. Instead of overhauling your entire schedule, begin with just one or two core habits and expand from there.

For example:

- If you want to develop a reading habit, start with just 5 minutes a day.
- If you want to exercise consistently, begin with 10 push-ups every morning.
- If you want to write every day, commit to one paragraph before breakfast.

By setting the bar low initially, you remove resistance and make it easy to follow through.

Step 3: Anchor New Habits to Existing Ones

A powerful way to make routines stick is through habit stacking—attaching a new habit to an existing one. This method takes advantage of patterns already established in your brain.

Examples of habit stacking:

- After I brush my teeth, I will drink a glass of water.
- After I pour my morning coffee, I will write down my top 5 priorities.
- After I finish lunch, I will go for a 5-minute walk.

By linking habits together, you reinforce consistency and integrate new behaviors naturally.

Step 4: Establish Clear Boundaries and Triggers

For your routines to become non-negotiable, you must remove ambiguity. Set clear rules and triggers that reinforce your habits.

- Time-Based Triggers: Set a fixed time for each routine (e.g., "I exercise at 7 AM").
- Action-Based Triggers: Link a habit to another action (e.g., "After every meeting, I write a summary").
- Environmental Triggers: Design your space to support good habits (e.g., "Keep a book on my nightstand to encourage nightly reading").

Step 5: Create Accountability and Track Progress

Accountability increases the likelihood of sticking to your routine. Tracking your habits helps build momentum and reinforces consistency.

Ways to stay accountable:

- Use a habit tracker to mark off daily progress.
- Find an accountability partner to check in with regularly.

- Commit publicly by sharing your goals with others.
- Reward yourself for consistency (but not for skipping days).

Seeing your progress visually strengthens your commitment and makes it harder to quit.

Step 6: Design Your Evening Routine for Success

Your evening routine plays a crucial role in setting up the next day for productivity. A strong evening habit eliminates decision fatigue and ensures you start each morning with clarity.

Effective evening routines include:

- Reviewing your Top 5 Priorities for the next day.
- Unplugging from screens at least 30 minutes before bed.
- Practicing gratitude or reflection.
- Ensuring 7-8 hours of quality sleep.

Step 7: Commit to Long-Term Consistency

The goal of non-negotiable daily routines isn't perfection—it's consistency. There will be days when you don't feel like following through, but the difference between high achievers and everyone else is that they show up even on tough days.

What to do when motivation dips:

- Reduce the effort but keep the habit (e.g., do 5 push-ups instead of 30).

- Remind yourself why you started.
- Use the "never miss twice" rule—if you miss a day, get back on track immediately.

Leveraging Momentum for Success

The Power of Momentum in Achievement

Momentum is the hidden force behind every great success story. Once you start moving in the right direction, it becomes easier to keep going. The key to sustained success isn't bursts of inspiration—it's harnessing momentum and ensuring continuous forward motion.

Momentum creates a cycle of progress. Small successes build confidence, confidence fuels action, and action generates more success. Whether in business, fitness, or personal development, momentum transforms effort into exponential growth.

Why Momentum Matters

Many people struggle to reach their goals because they rely on motivation, which fluctuates. Momentum, however, is reliable and self-sustaining. When you take consistent action, you eliminate the need for constant motivation and make progress feel natural.

Momentum is crucial because:

- It reduces resistance – The hardest part of any endeavor is getting started. Momentum makes future steps easier.

- It increases efficiency – Small wins build energy, leading to greater productivity.
- It reinforces habits – The more you repeat an action, the more ingrained it becomes.
- It eliminates decision fatigue – Progress becomes automatic rather than something you have to force.

Step 1: Start with Small, Consistent Wins

The best way to build momentum is by starting small. Many people set huge goals but struggle to follow through. Instead, focus on small, daily victories that create a foundation for long-term success.

How to build early momentum:

- Break big goals into tiny steps – Instead of writing a book, write 200 words per day.
- Use the "2-Minute Rule" – If a task takes less than two minutes, do it immediately.
- Celebrate small wins – Acknowledge every achievement, no matter how small.
- Stack habits for compound success – Pair new habits with existing ones to create automatic progress.

Small, consistent actions trigger a sense of accomplishment, making it easier to stay on track.

Step 2: Build Routines That Reinforce Progress

Routines are the fuel for momentum. When you systematize success, you remove the guesswork and make progress inevitable.

How to create momentum-building routines:

- Morning Routine: Start the day with productive actions (exercise, goal-setting, deep work).
- Work Flow Routine: Tackle the hardest or most impactful task first.
- Evening Routine: Reflect on the day's progress and set priorities for tomorrow.
- Review & Adjust Weekly: Regularly assess what's working and optimize accordingly.

Step 3: Use Feedback Loops to Accelerate Growth

Momentum thrives on feedback. When you track progress, adjust strategies, and learn from mistakes, you create a cycle of continuous improvement.

Ways to implement feedback loops:

- Track key metrics – Whether fitness goals, revenue growth, or personal milestones, measure progress.
- Analyze setbacks objectively – View failures as feedback, not defeat.
- Make small adjustments – Tweak systems to optimize performance without losing momentum.

- Seek external feedback – Mentors, coaches, or peers can provide valuable insights.

Step 4: Overcome Resistance and Keep Moving Forward

Even with strong momentum, obstacles will arise. The difference between those who succeed and those who don't is how they handle setbacks.

How to maintain momentum in the face of challenges:

- Embrace the "Never Miss Twice" Rule – If you miss a day, get back on track immediately.
- Refocus on your WHY – Remind yourself why the goal matters.
- Adjust, don't quit – If something isn't working, modify the approach rather than abandoning the goal.
- Eliminate friction – Reduce distractions and streamline your workflow.

Momentum isn't about never failing—it's about consistently getting back up and moving forward.

Step 5: Leverage the Compound Effect

Momentum is amplified by the compound effect, where small, consistent actions lead to massive results over time.

Ways to harness the compound effect:

- Daily 1% improvement – Small gains accumulate into massive progress.
- Master consistency over intensity – It's better to do a little every day than a lot occasionally.
- Let momentum drive bigger challenges – Once habits are established, tackle bigger goals.
- Stay patient – Compounding takes time, but the results are exponential.

The Compound Effect of Small Actions

The Power of Small, Consistent Actions

Most people overestimate what they can accomplish in a day but underestimate what they can achieve in a year. The secret to success isn't found in massive leaps but in the small, consistent actions that compound over time. This is known as the compound effect—a principle that has the power to transform your results in any area of life.

The compound effect states that tiny, seemingly insignificant choices, repeated consistently over time, lead to massive results. Whether you want to improve your health, business, relationships, or mindset, applying small positive actions daily will generate exponential growth over time.

Why Small Actions Matter More Than Big Changes

People often look for quick fixes and dramatic changes when pursuing goals. However, real, sustainable success is built on incremental progress. Here's why small actions are more powerful than big changes:

- Consistency Beats Intensity: A 1% improvement every day compounds into massive results over a year.
- Avoids Burnout: Small changes are sustainable, while drastic changes often lead to exhaustion and failure.
- Builds Confidence: Each small win reinforces belief in your ability to follow through.
- Creates Long-Term Success: Habits formed through small actions last, while drastic changes are usually short-lived.

The Math Behind the Compound Effect

Consider this: If you improve by just 1% every day, in one year, you won't just be 365% better—you'll be 37 times better due to the power of compounding.

Mathematically, it looks like this:

$$1.01^{365} = 37.78$$

That means that small, daily improvements don't add up—they multiply. Likewise, if you decline by 1% every day, you'll find yourself at almost zero by the end of the year.

$$0.99^{365} = 0.03$$

This highlights the power of consistent positive actions versus allowing negative habits to take over.

Real-Life Examples of the Compound Effect

The compound effect is evident in every aspect of life:

1. Health & Fitness – Doing just 10 push-ups a day doesn't seem like much, but over a year, that's 3,650 push-ups—a massive difference.
2. Wealth & Finances – Saving just $5 per day may seem trivial, but over ten years with compound interest, it becomes thousands of dollars.
3. Personal Growth – Reading 10 pages of a book daily results in over 12 books a year—a significant improvement in knowledge and mindset.
4. Relationships – Small daily gestures, like a kind text or a moment of appreciation, build stronger connections over time.

Step 1: Identify Small Actions with Big Impact

To apply the compound effect, start by identifying small, repeatable actions that align with your goals. Ask yourself:

- What daily habits, if maintained consistently, would lead to significant growth?
- What small improvements can I make that will add up over time?

Examples:

- If your goal is to get fit, commit to just 5 minutes of exercise daily.

- If your goal is financial freedom, save just $1 a day and increase over time.
- If your goal is learning, read or listen to educational content for 10 minutes daily.

Step 2: Build Consistency and Discipline

The key to harnessing the compound effect is sticking with small habits long enough for them to generate momentum. This requires discipline and commitment.

Tips to stay consistent:

- Use Habit Stacking: Attach a new habit to an existing one (e.g., after brushing your teeth, do 10 push-ups).
- Track Progress: Use a habit tracker or journal to measure consistency.
- Eliminate Decision Fatigue: Make small actions automatic by scheduling them into your daily routine.
- Stay Accountable: Share your progress with a friend or mentor.

Step 3: Leverage the Ripple Effect

The compound effect doesn't just influence your direct actions—it creates a ripple effect that impacts every area of your life.

For example:

- Improving physical health leads to more energy, confidence, and productivity.
- Developing financial discipline creates more freedom and reduces stress.
- Strengthening relationships improves emotional well-being and resilience.

Every small action compounds into bigger changes than you initially expect.

Step 4: Avoid Negative Compounding

Just as small positive actions create success, small negative habits compound into failure if left unchecked.

Examples of negative compounding:

- Skipping workouts leads to loss of fitness over time.
- Mindless spending adds up to thousands of dollars wasted.
- Consistently poor food choices result in declining health.
- Neglecting relationships leads to disconnection and resentment.

Being aware of negative compounding allows you to course-correct before habits spiral out of control.

Step 5: Celebrate Progress and Trust the Process

The compound effect requires patience. Results won't be immediate, but they will be inevitable. The key is to trust the process and recognize that even when changes seem small, they are building momentum toward something much bigger.

Ways to reinforce progress:

- Celebrate small wins – Acknowledge every small milestone to stay motivated.
- Visualize long-term impact – Remind yourself how today's effort contributes to future success.
- Stay committed to the process – Trust that consistency will bring rewards even if you don't see immediate results.

Summary of Part 2: The Strategy

Success doesn't happen by accident—it's the result of a structured approach that turns ambition into action. Part 2: The Strategy provides the framework to bridge the gap between setting goals and actually achieving them. By implementing a system that prioritizes the right actions, builds momentum, and creates lasting habits, you set yourself up for long-term success.

Reverse Engineering Success

Most people set goals but struggle with execution because they don't break their ambitions down into actionable steps. Reverse engineering teaches us to start with the end goal in mind and work backward, defining clear milestones and tasks. The 90-day sprint approach helps maintain focus by setting short-term targets that build towards long-term success. Instead of relying on willpower alone, designing a system that aligns with your strengths ensures that progress becomes predictable and repeatable.

The Topify Quadrants: Prioritizing What Truly Matters

Not all actions contribute equally to success. Many people get stuck in busyness rather than progress because they fail to distinguish between essential tasks and distractions. The Topify Quadrants provide a simple but powerful method to categorize actions into four key areas:

1. Essential Tasks – The core activities that drive direct results.
2. Growth Tasks – Investments in learning and skill-building that create future opportunities.
3. Delegation Tasks – Responsibilities that can be handed off to free up time for higher-value work.
4. Elimination Tasks – Low-value distractions that drain time without meaningful returns.

By applying this framework, decision-making becomes effortless, and focus is directed toward high-impact work.

The Science of Habit Stacking

Big goals are achieved through small, daily actions that accumulate over time. The concept of habit stacking simplifies behavior change by linking new habits to existing routines, making them easier to adopt. Building non-negotiable daily routines ensures that success becomes a byproduct of consistency rather than motivation. The key is to leverage momentum so that each positive action reinforces the next, creating a compounding effect of growth.

The Compound Effect: How Small Actions Lead to Big Results

The final component of The Strategy is understanding how the smallest actions, repeated consistently, create exponential success. Whether it's improving by 1% each day, making incremental progress in fitness, finances, or career, the compound effect ensures that daily discipline leads to transformational outcomes. By focusing on execution rather than perfection, and trusting the process, long-term results become inevitable.

Part 3: The Execution

A powerful vision and a well-structured strategy mean nothing without execution. The difference between those who succeed and those who remain stuck in the cycle of unfulfilled potential is consistent daily action. Execution is where ideas become reality, where momentum turns into results, and where progress compounds into long-term success.

Yet, most people struggle with execution—not because they lack ambition, but because they lack a clear system for taking action. Distractions, procrastination, and inefficient work habits create roadblocks that stall progress. The key to winning is not just working hard—it's working smart and executing with precision.

This section of the book focuses on transforming intentions into consistent action. You'll learn how to design your perfect day using the Topify Planner, master the mental shifts required to overcome resistance, and implement a powerful reflection system that keeps you on track.

What You'll Discover in This Section:

- Chapter 6: The Daily Plan That Wins – A step-by-step guide to designing your most productive day. You'll learn how to structure your time using morning mindset rituals, action blocks, and daily review cycles to ensure you're not just busy, but genuinely productive.
- Chapter 7: Overcoming Resistance – Procrastination and self-doubt kill execution. Here, you'll discover the psychology of resistance, how to rewire your brain for

action, and strategies to push through when motivation fails.
- Chapter 8: The 45-Second Reset – Execution isn't about perfection; it's about continuous improvement. The Topify Reflection Method teaches you how micro-adjustments can lead to massive success and how to use a simple evening review to lock in progress daily.

By the end of this section, you'll have a clear, repeatable system for execution that eliminates hesitation, keeps you focused, and ensures that your goals don't remain dreams—they become achievements.

Chapter 6: The Daily Plan That Wins

The foundation of success isn't found in sporadic bursts of motivation or in the pursuit of perfection—it's built through a structured, intentional daily plan. Every highly successful individual follows a system that keeps them on track, minimizes distractions, and ensures they are making meaningful progress toward their goals.

Yet, most people start their day in reaction mode, immediately responding to emails, scrolling through notifications, or diving into tasks without a clear sense of direction. This leads to days filled with busyness but lacking productivity. The key to consistent progress is designing a daily plan that prioritizes high-impact work while maintaining energy and focus.

This chapter is about creating a repeatable success formula for each day—one that ensures you execute with clarity, efficiency, and purpose. You'll learn how to structure your time effectively, eliminate distractions, and design a workflow that maximizes productivity without burnout.

Why a Daily Plan is Non-Negotiable

Without a clear daily structure, success is left to chance. A well-planned day provides:

- Clarity: You start the day knowing exactly what to focus on.
- Momentum: You build small wins that compound over time.

- Efficiency: You eliminate wasted effort on low-value tasks.
- Balance: You optimize energy to stay productive without burning out.

What You'll Learn in This Chapter:

- How to design your perfect day using the Topify Planner
- The power of action blocks and time segmentation to eliminate distractions
- How to separate busyness from productivity so every effort moves you forward
- The importance of daily review cycles to refine and optimize your approach

A strong daily plan isn't rigid—it's flexible enough to adapt to challenges while ensuring you stay in control of your progress. By mastering daily execution, you turn success into an inevitability rather than a possibility.

Designing Your Perfect Day with the Topify Productivity Planner

The Power of a Well-Designed Day

Success isn't about luck or talent—it's about how you structure your day. The most accomplished individuals have one thing in common: they don't leave their daily success to chance. Instead, they follow a structured plan that aligns their actions with their most important goals.

The Topify Productivity Planner is designed to help you create a perfect day—one where you focus on what truly matters, eliminate distractions, and make meaningful progress. By using a proven system, you take control of your time, energy, and focus, ensuring that each day moves you closer to your long-term goals.

Step 1: Start with the Morning Mindset

The way you begin your day sets the tone for everything that follows. A strong morning routine eliminates decision fatigue and puts you in the right frame of mind for productivity.

Key elements of a productive morning:

- Gratitude and Reflection – Take a moment to appreciate progress and set a positive tone.
- Clear Intentions – Define what success looks like for the day.
- Mindfulness or Movement – Engage in meditation, exercise, or stretching to energize the body and mind.
- Review Your Top 5 Priorities – Use the Topify Planner to clarify the most impactful actions for the day.

By starting with clarity and purpose, you ensure that your day is guided by intentional action rather than external distractions.

Step 2: The Topify Action Blocks

The biggest productivity killer is task switching—jumping from one task to another without focus. The Topify Planner introduces Action Blocks, structured time periods dedicated to deep work.

How to use Action Blocks effectively:

1. Define your focus tasks – Choose 1-3 high-impact tasks that align with your goals.
2. Set a specific timeframe – Allocate 60-90 minutes per block to work without interruptions.
3. Eliminate distractions – Turn off notifications, close unnecessary tabs, and create a distraction-free workspace.
4. Use time tracking – Monitor how long each task takes and refine your approach over time.

By structuring your day around focused work periods, you get more done in less time, freeing up energy for strategic thinking and creative work.

Step 3: Prioritizing Effectively with the Top 1 Task

Not all tasks are created equal. The Topify Planner emphasizes the Top 1 Task Method, ensuring that the most important work gets done first.

How to identify your Top 1 Task:

- Ask: *What single task, if completed today, will make the biggest impact?*
- Choose a task that aligns with your long-term goals.
- Tackle it first thing in the morning while your energy is highest.

By making progress on the most critical task early, you set the momentum for the rest of the day.

Step 4: The Difference Between Busy and Productive

Many people mistake busyness for productivity. Checking emails, attending endless meetings, and responding to messages may feel productive, but they often don't contribute to meaningful progress.

The Topify Planner helps you differentiate between:

- High-impact tasks (strategic work, creative projects, revenue-generating actions)
- Low-value tasks (excessive meetings, reactive emails, unnecessary admin work)

By focusing on what truly matters, you reclaim control over your schedule and eliminate time-wasting activities.

Step 5: The Midday Reset for Sustained Performance

Energy and focus naturally dip throughout the day. Instead of powering through with diminishing efficiency, use a midday reset to recharge.

Simple ways to reset midday:

- Step away from work and take a 5-10 minute movement break.
- Practice deep breathing or a short meditation to reset mental clarity.
- Review your progress and adjust priorities for the afternoon.

By integrating small energy-boosting habits, you maintain peak performance throughout the day.

Step 6: The Evening Review for Continuous Improvement

Your day isn't complete without a reflection process. The Topify Planner includes an Evening Review, a simple but powerful way to assess what worked, what didn't, and what to improve for tomorrow.

Key questions for your Evening Review:

- What were today's biggest wins?
- Did I complete my Top 1 Task?
- What obstacles did I face, and how can I adjust tomorrow?
- What am I grateful for?

By taking a few minutes to analyze and refine your approach, you ensure that each day is better than the last.

Morning Mindset, Action Blocks, and Review Cycles

The Power of a Strong Morning Mindset

Your morning mindset sets the tone for the entire day. How you start your morning determines your level of focus, energy, and productivity. If you begin your day feeling rushed, reactive, or unprepared, you'll likely carry that energy into every task. On the other hand, an intentional morning routine primes your mind for success and execution.

A strong morning mindset isn't about how early you wake up; it's about what you do with your first hour of the day. High achievers structure their mornings around clarity, priority-setting, and energy management.

Step 1: Setting a Clear Intention

Start your morning by defining what success looks like for the day. Ask yourself:

- *What's my primary focus today?*
- *What is the single most important thing I must complete?*
- *How do I want to show up today—mentally, emotionally, and physically?*

Journaling or using a productivity planner for a quick 5-minute morning intention exercise helps solidify your mindset and prevents aimless decision-making throughout the day.

Step 2: Priming Your Energy

Your body fuels your brain. If you neglect your physical well-being in the morning, your cognitive performance will suffer. Implement these quick energy-boosting habits:

- Hydration – Start the day with a glass of water to wake up your system.
- Movement – Stretch, do light exercise, or walk to stimulate blood flow and alertness.
- Mindfulness – Engage in breathing exercises, meditation, or visualization to cultivate mental clarity.

These actions take less than 15 minutes but can significantly enhance your energy levels and focus throughout the day.

Action Blocks: Structuring Your Work for Maximum Productivity

Many people mistake busyness for productivity. The most effective performers don't just work harder—they work smarter by structuring their day with Action Blocks.

Action Blocks are designated periods of deep focus, during which you tackle one high-priority task at a time without distractions. Instead of constantly switching between tasks, which drains mental energy, this approach allows for peak efficiency and output.

Step 1: Define Your Action Blocks

Identify 3-4 key time slots throughout the day when you'll work in deep focus. Each block should:

- Be dedicated to a single high-impact task (e.g., writing, strategic planning, deep learning).
- Last between 60-90 minutes to match the brain's optimal focus cycles.
- Be protected from interruptions (e.g., phone on silent, email notifications off, work in a quiet space).

Step 2: The 90-Minute Rule

Science shows that the brain operates best in 90-minute ultradian cycles. Instead of working non-stop, structure your work into 90-minute focus blocks followed by short recovery breaks.

An ideal Action Block schedule might look like this:

- 9:00-10:30 AM: Deep work on your highest-priority task.
- 10:30-10:45 AM: Break (walk, hydrate, stretch, breathe).
- 10:45 AM-12:15 PM: Focus on the next priority task.
- 12:15-1:00 PM: Lunch and full mental reset.

By repeating this cycle throughout the day, you maintain energy, avoid burnout, and maximize productivity.

Step 3: The Rule of Three

To prevent overwhelm, define your Top 3 Priorities for the day. These should be the most important, high-impact tasks that will move you closer to your goals.

Each Action Block should focus on one of these priorities, ensuring that progress is deliberate and meaningful.

Review Cycles: The Key to Consistent Growth

At the end of the day, many people feel exhausted but uncertain about whether they actually made progress. That's why a review cycle is crucial—it locks in lessons, progress, and insights for continuous improvement.

Step 1: Midday Reset

Halfway through your day, take five minutes to review your progress and adjust if needed.

- Have I completed at least one of my top priorities?
- What obstacles or distractions have I encountered?
- Do I need to reallocate focus for the afternoon?

A midday reset ensures that you don't drift off track and allows for adjustments in real time.

Step 2: The Evening Reflection

Before ending the day, take 10 minutes to conduct an evening review. This simple practice helps close the loop on your progress and prepares you for the next day.

Ask yourself:

- *What were my biggest wins today?*
- *Did I complete my Top 1 Task?*
- *What challenged me, and how will I adjust?*
- *What will be my #1 priority tomorrow?*

Documenting these reflections helps reinforce habitual success patterns and eliminates the stress of feeling unprepared for the next day.

The Formula for Daily Success

By combining morning mindset, structured action blocks, and review cycles, you create a powerful execution system that ensures productivity without burnout.

1. Morning Mindset → Aligns your focus and energy for the day.
2. Action Blocks → Structures your work for deep, meaningful progress.
3. Review Cycles → Reinforces learning and keeps your execution sharp.

This method transforms your daily approach from random effort to structured success. By designing each day with intention, you remove guesswork, increase efficiency, and accelerate long-term achievements.

The Difference Between Busy and Productive

Why Being Busy Isn't the Same as Being Productive

In today's fast-paced world, being busy has become a status symbol. People wear their packed schedules like a badge of honor, equating a full calendar with success. But busyness doesn't always translate to productivity. In fact, many people spend their days feeling overwhelmed, jumping from task to task, yet making little meaningful progress.

Being busy means you're doing a lot of things. Being productive means you're doing the right things. The key to achieving real success is learning how to distinguish between activity and impact—focusing on actions that drive meaningful results instead of just filling time.

1. Understanding Busyness vs. Productivity

Let's break it down:

Busy People	Productive People
React to everything as it comes	Work with clear priorities
Fill their schedule with meetings and tasks	Focus on high-impact activities
Check emails and messages constantly	Time-block communication to avoid distractions
Multitask frequently	Single-task for deeper focus
Feel exhausted but accomplish little	Feel accomplished with fewer, meaningful tasks
Work long hours without direction	Get more done in less time through efficiency

Productivity isn't about doing more—it's about doing what matters most.

2. Signs You're Stuck in the Busyness Trap

How do you know if you're simply busy rather than truly productive? If you experience any of these, you might be falling into the busyness trap:

- You start your day without a clear plan and spend most of your time reacting to emails and messages.

- Your to-do list is endless, but you rarely finish high-priority tasks.
- You jump from task to task but don't make meaningful progress on big projects.
- You feel exhausted but unfulfilled at the end of the day.
- You struggle to set boundaries, constantly taking on more than you can handle.

Recognizing these patterns is the first step toward shifting from busyness to productivity.

3. The Power of Prioritization

One of the biggest differences between busy and productive people is how they prioritize tasks.

The Eisenhower Matrix

A powerful tool for prioritization is the Eisenhower Matrix, which helps categorize tasks based on urgency and importance:

Urgency vs. Importance	Urgent & Important	Not Urgent but Important	Urgent but Not Important	Neither Urgent nor Important
What It Means	Must be done immediately	High-value tasks that require planning	Distractions that feel important but aren't	Time-wasters that add no value
Examples	Crisis management, deadlines	Strategic planning, learning, deep work	Interruptions, unnecessary meetings	Mindless scrolling, unproductive activities
Action	Do it now	Schedule it	Delegate it	Eliminate it

Productive people spend most of their time in the 'Not Urgent but Important' quadrant, working proactively on tasks that drive long-term success.

4. Eliminating Time-Wasting Activities

To become more productive, you need to identify and eliminate time-wasters that contribute to busyness but not results.

Common Time-Wasters & How to Fix Them:

1. Checking Email Constantly → Set specific times to check email instead of reacting all day.

2. Excessive Meetings → Only attend meetings with a clear agenda and defined outcomes.
3. Social Media Scrolling → Use website blockers or set limits on social apps.
4. Multitasking → Focus on one task at a time for deeper concentration.
5. Lack of Boundaries → Learn to say no to non-essential commitments.

By eliminating distractions, you free up time for tasks that actually matter.

5. The Art of Deep Work

A major factor in productivity is the ability to focus deeply. Busy people spread their attention thin, while productive people engage in 'deep work'—uninterrupted focus on meaningful tasks.

How to Cultivate Deep Work:

- Schedule Focus Blocks – Allocate 60-90 minute sessions for uninterrupted work.
- Turn Off Notifications – Remove digital distractions during deep work periods.
- Work in a Distraction-Free Environment – Design your space to support focus.
- Use the Pomodoro Technique – Work for 25-45 minutes, then take short breaks.

Deep work allows you to accomplish more in two focused hours than an entire day of shallow, distracted work.

6. Measuring Success Differently

Busy people measure success by how much they do. Productive people measure success by what they accomplish.

Shift Your Metrics for Success:

- Instead of counting tasks completed, track meaningful progress on key projects.
- Instead of working longer hours, focus on doing high-impact work efficiently.
- Instead of saying yes to everything, learn to protect your time and energy.

Success isn't about being the busiest person in the room—it's about creating real impact with the time you have.

7. How to Transition from Busy to Productive

If you find yourself caught in the busyness cycle, it's not too late to shift gears. Here's how:

1. Start each day with clarity – Define your Top 3 Priorities before checking emails or messages.
2. Use time-blocking – Structure your day around focused work, meetings, and rest.
3. Batch similar tasks – Handle emails, calls, and admin work in designated blocks to avoid constant interruptions.

4. Protect deep work time – Create non-negotiable focus sessions for high-value tasks.
5. Review and adjust weekly – Assess progress and refine strategies to maximize effectiveness.

By implementing these shifts, you'll stop feeling overwhelmed and start experiencing real progress.

Chapter 7: Overcoming Resistance

Every ambitious goal comes with an invisible force working against it—resistance. It shows up as procrastination, self-doubt, distractions, and fear. No matter how motivated or disciplined you are, resistance will always try to hold you back from taking meaningful action. The real question is not whether you will face resistance but how you will overcome it.

Resistance often disguises itself as logical excuses: "I'll start tomorrow," "I need more time to prepare," or "I don't feel ready." But at its core, resistance is a mechanism designed to keep you comfortable, safe, and within familiar territory. The problem? Success lives outside of your comfort zone.

The difference between those who achieve their goals and those who don't isn't intelligence, talent, or luck—it's the ability to consistently push past resistance and take action, even when it feels uncomfortable. Mastering execution is about learning how to break through internal barriers and develop a mindset of action.

This chapter will teach you:

- The psychology of procrastination and why resistance occurs.
- How to rewire your brain for execution instead of hesitation.
- The best strategies to take action even when motivation is low.

By the end of this chapter, you will have the tools to turn resistance into fuel, ensuring that inaction is no longer an option. Progress will no longer be dependent on fleeting motivation, but instead built on a system of consistent execution. Let's dive in and learn how to break through the walls that stand between you and success.

The Psychology of Procrastination

Understanding Procrastination: The Root Cause of Inaction

Procrastination is one of the most persistent obstacles to success. It's not about laziness or lack of ambition—it's a psychological battle between short-term comfort and long-term goals. When we procrastinate, we aren't just delaying tasks; we are engaging in a self-sabotaging behavior that can have long-term consequences on our productivity, self-esteem, and overall well-being.

Why Do We Procrastinate? The Science Behind It

At its core, procrastination is driven by two opposing forces in the brain:

1. The Prefrontal Cortex – The rational part of the brain that plans, sets goals, and makes logical decisions.
2. The Limbic System – The emotional, impulsive part of the brain that seeks instant gratification and avoids discomfort.

When faced with a task that requires effort, the limbic system triggers avoidance behavior, preferring an immediate reward (e.g., watching Netflix, scrolling social media) rather than engaging in a challenging but meaningful activity. This is why procrastination feels like relief in the short term—but leads to stress and regret in the long term.

The Different Types of Procrastination

Not all procrastination is the same. Understanding why you delay tasks can help you develop strategies to overcome it.

1. Perfectionist Procrastination

- Fear of making mistakes or not meeting high expectations leads to avoidance.
- The person believes, "If I can't do it perfectly, I shouldn't do it at all."
- Solution: Adopt a progress-over-perfection mindset. Start small and refine as you go.

2. Fear-Based Procrastination

- Avoiding tasks due to fear of failure, rejection, or judgment.
- Common in high-stakes situations like career decisions or creative projects.
- Solution: Reframe fear as a natural part of growth and take small steps forward.

3. Task Aversion Procrastination

- Occurs when the task is boring, tedious, or overwhelming.
- The brain seeks out more enjoyable distractions.
- Solution: Break the task into smaller, manageable steps and pair it with rewards.

4. Last-Minute Rush Procrastination

- Some people thrive under pressure and delay work until the last moment.
- Can lead to high stress, lower quality results, and burnout.
- Solution: Set artificial deadlines to create urgency without unnecessary stress.

5. Decision Fatigue Procrastination

- Avoiding tasks because too many choices lead to analysis paralysis.
- Overthinking options prevents action.
- Solution: Limit choices and commit to a decision without overanalyzing.

The Emotional Cycle of Procrastination

Procrastination follows a predictable emotional pattern:

1. The Trigger – A task feels uncomfortable or overwhelming.
2. Avoidance Behavior – You choose a distraction to escape discomfort.
3. Temporary Relief – You feel good in the moment, avoiding stress.
4. Guilt and Anxiety – As the deadline approaches, stress builds.
5. Panic and Action – You rush to complete the task under pressure.
6. Repeat Cycle – Without intervention, this pattern continues indefinitely.

To break the cycle, you must disrupt the loop before avoidance sets in.

Strategies to Overcome Procrastination

1. The 5-Minute Rule

One of the simplest ways to beat procrastination is by using the 5-minute rule: Tell yourself you'll work on a task for just five minutes. Once you start, the hardest part is over, and momentum often carries you forward.

2. Implementation Intentions

Set clear action plans using the "If-Then" formula:

- *If I finish breakfast, then I will write for 30 minutes.*
- *If it's 3 PM, then I will respond to pending emails.*

This removes ambiguity and creates automatic action triggers.

3. Time Blocking and the Pomodoro Technique

- Time Blocking – Schedule work sessions in advance to create commitment.
- Pomodoro Technique – Work in 25-minute sprints followed by short breaks.

4. Accountability and Public Commitment

- Tell a friend or mentor about your task and set a deadline.
- Use productivity apps or group challenges to track progress.

5. Reframing the Task

Instead of focusing on how difficult or tedious a task is, ask yourself:

- *What benefits will I gain from completing this?*
- *How will my future self feel if I take action now?*

Shifting focus from difficulty to benefits and outcomes can make tasks feel more rewarding.

How to Stay Consistent and Beat Procrastination for Good

1. Build Routines – Create daily habits that eliminate the need for decision-making.

2. Lower Resistance – Start with smaller, manageable steps instead of tackling an entire project at once.
3. Remove Distractions – Identify what derails your focus and eliminate it from your workspace.
4. Reward Progress – Celebrate small wins to reinforce positive behavior.
5. Adopt the Identity of an Action-Taker – Instead of saying, *I struggle with procrastination*, say *I take action even when I don't feel like it*.

Rewiring Your Brain for Execution

The Science of Taking Action

Most people know what they need to do to succeed, yet they struggle with execution. Why? Because their brain is wired for comfort, not action. The human brain naturally seeks the path of least resistance, favoring short-term gratification over long-term achievement. However, through neuroscience-backed strategies, you can rewire your brain to prioritize execution over procrastination and transform yourself into someone who consistently follows through on their goals.

Understanding the Brain's Role in Execution

Your ability to execute is largely influenced by two key parts of the brain:

- The Prefrontal Cortex – The logical part of the brain responsible for decision-making, planning, and goal-setting.
- The Limbic System – The emotional, primitive part of the brain that seeks comfort, avoids pain, and craves instant gratification.

When execution is difficult, it's because the limbic system is overpowering the prefrontal cortex, leading to procrastination, avoidance, and distractions. The goal is to strengthen the prefrontal cortex so it has more control over decision-making and action.

Step 1: Train Your Brain to Overcome Resistance

Resistance to execution often stems from fear, uncertainty, or mental overwhelm. The key is to rewire your brain by making action automatic rather than something you have to force yourself to do.

The 5-Second Rule

Coined by Mel Robbins, this method trains the brain to take action before resistance kicks in. When you feel hesitation, count down from 5 and immediately take action—before your brain can talk you out of it. This interrupts the default procrastination pattern and rewires your brain to act faster.

The 2-Minute Rule

If a task takes less than two minutes, do it immediately. Small actions create momentum, and by repeatedly executing minor tasks, you train your brain to associate action with ease instead of resistance.

Daily Micro-Wins

Set small, achievable goals every day. Completing even one tiny task daily builds neural pathways that associate execution with success, reinforcing action-oriented behavior.

Step 2: Reduce Friction and Make Execution Effortless

One reason people struggle with execution is because their environment or workflow is filled with friction—small obstacles that make taking action more difficult. Removing these friction points makes it easier for your brain to default to execution mode.

Eliminate Choice Paralysis

Too many choices overwhelm the brain and cause decision fatigue. Reduce options by pre-planning your day:

- Choose one key priority for the day.
- Decide on your tasks the night before.
- Automate small decisions (e.g., wear the same type of outfit daily like Steve Jobs did).

Create an Action-First Environment

Your surroundings shape your behavior. Design your environment to support execution:

- Keep your workspace clean and distraction-free.

- Place visual reminders of goals where you can see them.
- Remove temptations (e.g., keep your phone in another room while working).

Step 3: Reprogram Your Brain with New Associations

Your brain is wired to avoid pain and seek pleasure. By changing how you associate action with emotions, you can train your brain to see execution as rewarding rather than stressful.

Use Dopamine to Your Advantage

Dopamine is the neurotransmitter linked to motivation and reward. Instead of waiting for dopamine from external rewards, generate it yourself through intentional behaviors:

- Gamify your progress – Use checklists or streak-tracking to trigger dopamine from small wins.
- Celebrate micro-successes – Acknowledge small accomplishments to reinforce execution.
- Use immediate gratification – Reward yourself after completing important tasks (e.g., take a short walk after finishing deep work).

Reframe Painful Tasks as Opportunities

Instead of saying, *I have to do this*, reframe it as *I get to do this*. Changing your language shifts the way your brain perceives tasks, reducing resistance and increasing motivation.

Step 4: Strengthen the Execution Muscle Through Repetition

Execution is a habit, and like any habit, it must be built through repetition and reinforcement. Here's how:

Commit to Non-Negotiable Actions

- Identify 3 daily non-negotiable actions related to your goals.
- Treat them as essential—just like brushing your teeth.
- Stick to them even when you don't feel like it (discipline over motivation).

Develop a "Now" Mentality

- Train yourself to start tasks immediately, rather than postponing them.
- Adopt the rule: *If it's on my list today, I do it today.*
- View execution as part of your identity: *I am someone who takes action.*

The 1% Improvement Rule

- Commit to improving execution by just 1% each day.
- Tiny, daily improvements compound into massive long-term results.
- Focus on consistency over perfection.

Step 5: Manage Energy for Maximum Execution Power

Execution isn't just about willpower—it's about energy management. If your brain and body are drained, execution becomes exponentially harder.

Optimize Your Sleep and Nutrition

- Get 7-8 hours of sleep to support cognitive function.
- Eat brain-fueling foods like protein, healthy fats, and complex carbs.
- Stay hydrated—dehydration reduces mental clarity and focus.

Use Strategic Breaks

Pushing yourself to work non-stop leads to burnout. Instead, follow a structured break schedule to maintain execution power:

- Work in 90-minute focus cycles, then take a 10-minute break.
- Step away from screens and move your body to refresh your mind.

How to Win When Motivation Fails

The Myth of Constant Motivation

Most people believe that motivation is the key to success. They wait for inspiration to strike before taking action, assuming that high achievers operate from a place of constant enthusiasm. But the truth is, even the most successful individuals don't rely on motivation to get things done. They rely on systems, habits, and discipline.

Motivation is fleeting. It fluctuates based on mood, environment, and external circumstances. If you only take action when you feel motivated, you'll make slow, inconsistent progress. Winning in life and business isn't about feeling motivated—it's about executing even when you don't feel like it.

This chapter explores practical strategies to ensure that you keep moving forward, no matter how uninspired or unmotivated you feel.

Step 1: Understand Why Motivation Fails

To beat the trap of relying on motivation, you must first understand why it fades.

1. The Brain's Preference for Comfort

Your brain is wired for survival, not achievement. It seeks immediate gratification and avoids discomfort. That's why watching Netflix feels easier than going to the gym, and scrolling social media feels easier than working on your goals.

2. The "All or Nothing" Mentality

People often believe they must be 100% motivated to start something. If they feel even slightly unmotivated, they assume it's not the right time to act. This mindset is a major productivity killer.

3. Emotional States Are Unreliable

Motivation is tied to how you feel in the moment. If you had a bad day, didn't sleep well, or received negative feedback, your motivation will likely plummet. If you only take action when you "feel like it," you'll be inconsistent.

Solution: Understand that motivation is not required for action. Action creates motivation, not the other way around.

Step 2: Create a System That Works Without Motivation

The best way to stay productive even when motivation is low is to remove the need for motivation altogether. This is done by implementing systems that make action automatic.

1. Commit to a Non-Negotiable Routine

- High achievers don't wake up and decide if they'll work out or if they'll write today. They have a system that removes choice.
- Create a routine where the most important actions happen at the same time every day, making execution automatic.

2. Use the 5-Second Rule

- When you feel hesitation, count down from five and take action immediately.
- This short-circuits the brain's resistance and prevents overthinking.

3. Set an "Action Minimum"

- If a task feels overwhelming, commit to just 5 minutes of action.
- Often, once you start, you'll keep going. This is called activation energy—the hardest part is getting started.

Step 3: Build Discipline as a Muscle

Discipline is the ability to take action regardless of how you feel. It's stronger than motivation because it doesn't rely on temporary emotions.

1. Start Small, Build Consistency

- Don't aim for perfection—aim for consistency.
- It's better to do 10 minutes of focused work every day than to work for 3 hours once a week when you feel motivated.

2. Make It Easy to Start

- Remove barriers to action. Prepare your environment for success.
    - Want to work out? Lay out your gym clothes the night before.
    - Want to write daily? Keep a notepad or open document ready.

3. Eliminate Decision Fatigue

- The more choices you have to make, the more likely you are to procrastinate.
- Plan your day the night before so you wake up knowing exactly what to do.

Step 4: Use External Accountability

If you struggle with self-motivation, create external systems that force you to follow through.

1. Public Commitment

- Tell someone your goal and give them permission to hold you accountable.
- Example: Announce on social media that you'll run 5 miles a week, making it harder to back out.

2. Accountability Partners

- Pair up with someone who has similar goals. Check in daily or weekly.

3. Pre-Commitment Contracts

- Create a consequence for not following through.
- Example: Give a friend $50 and tell them to keep it if you don't complete your task.

Step 5: Leverage the Power of Momentum

Momentum makes execution easier. The more you take action, the less effort is required to continue.

1. Focus on Daily Wins

- Even small wins build confidence and create momentum.
- Keep a "Wins Journal" to track daily progress.

2. Never Miss Twice

- Missing one day is inevitable. Missing two days in a row is a habit breaker.
- If you miss a workout, writing session, or business task, make sure the next day is a success.

3. Use the Identity Shift Trick

- Instead of saying, *I need to get motivated to work out*, say, *I am the type of person who never skips a workout.*
- Identity-based habits create long-term consistency.

Chapter 8: The 45-Second Reset

Success isn't about working harder—it's about working smarter. The greatest performers, entrepreneurs, and leaders don't push through exhaustion or rely on constant motivation. Instead, they understand the power of quick, intentional resets to refocus their energy and regain control over their day. This is where the 45-Second Reset comes in.

In a world filled with distractions, stress, and constant demands on our attention, it's easy to become overwhelmed, lose focus, or spiral into unproductive behaviors. Many people think they need an hour-long break, a vacation, or a perfect routine to get back on track, but the truth is, small moments of intentional reflection and adjustment can be just as powerful.

The 45-Second Reset is a micro-strategy designed to help you quickly regain momentum, reframe your mindset, and break through mental blocks in under a minute. Whether you're battling procrastination, frustration, or just need a mental refresh, this method provides a simple but effective way to snap back into action.

In this chapter, you'll learn:

- The science behind micro-resets and why they work.
- How to use the 45-Second Reset to instantly shift your focus and energy.
- Practical techniques to apply this method anytime, anywhere.

- How small resets compound over time to create massive productivity gains.

By the end of this chapter, you'll have a powerful tool to prevent burnout, stay on track, and consistently perform at your best—all by mastering the art of quick resets.

The Topify Reflection Method

The Power of Reflection in Achievement

High achievers don't just work hard—they work smart. They don't simply focus on doing more; they focus on learning from what they've done. This is where The Topify Reflection Method comes in. It's a simple yet powerful system that ensures you're not just moving but moving in the right direction.

Many people fail to reach their goals not because they lack effort but because they don't take time to reflect. Without reflection, mistakes are repeated, successes go unrecognized, and progress stalls. The Topify Reflection Method provides a structured way to review, adjust, and improve, ensuring consistent, compounding growth over time.

Why Reflection is the Missing Key to Growth

Most productivity methods focus on planning and execution, but they often ignore the third crucial component: reflection. Without reflection:

- You may continue inefficient habits without realizing it.
- You won't know what's working and what's not.
- You're more likely to burn out without course correction.

The Topify Reflection Method is built around the idea that progress is a cycle, not a straight line. It helps you close the loop on your efforts so you can make smarter, more informed decisions about your next steps.

Step 1: The Daily Micro-Reflection (5 Minutes)

At the end of each day, take five minutes to ask yourself key questions. This micro-reflection helps you process what happened during the day, recognize wins, and adjust for tomorrow.

Questions to Ask:

1. *What was my biggest win today?*
2. *What was my biggest challenge?*
3. *What could I have done differently?*
4. *What is my #1 priority for tomorrow?*

By taking a few moments to reflect, you solidify lessons learned and set yourself up for better decision-making the next day.

Step 2: The Weekly Reset (30 Minutes)

A weekly reflection gives you a broader perspective on your progress and prevents getting stuck in daily busyness without real movement.

How to Conduct a Weekly Reset:

- Review Your Top 5 Priorities: Are they aligned with your long-term goals?
- Assess What Worked and What Didn't: Identify what's driving results and what's wasting time.
- Analyze Energy Levels: When did you feel most focused? When did you struggle?
- Plan Adjustments: Based on your insights, refine your plan for the upcoming week.

This process ensures that each week is a building block for greater productivity and success.

Step 3: The Monthly Review (1 Hour)

A monthly review allows for deeper insights and helps you recognize trends that impact long-term success.

Key Areas to Review:

- Goal Progress: Are you on track with your bigger objectives?
- Challenges Overcome: What obstacles did you navigate successfully?
- Lessons Learned: What insights can you apply moving forward?
- Habits and Routines: Which ones served you? Which ones need adjustment?

The monthly reflection acts as a checkpoint to ensure you're aligned with your long-term vision and not just moving for the sake of movement.

Step 4: The Quarterly Growth Audit

A quarterly review is where true transformation happens. By stepping back and analyzing progress over a longer timeframe, you gain valuable insights into your personal growth and overall strategy.

How to Conduct a Quarterly Growth Audit:

- Compare Progress to Goals: Are you ahead, behind, or on track?
- Identify Patterns: Are there recurring challenges or successes?
- Realign Priorities: Are your current goals still relevant?
- Set New Benchmarks: Define what success looks like for the next quarter.

This step helps prevent drifting and ensures that every action you take is deliberate and impactful.

The Secret to Making Reflection Work: Actionable Adjustments

Reflection without action is useless. The Topify Reflection Method is designed not just to analyze but to refine.

After each reflection session, create an Action Adjustment Plan, where you:

1. Identify one small improvement you can make immediately.
2. Commit to an action that ensures progress based on your insights.
3. Track your adjustments to measure effectiveness over time.

These small refinements compound over time, leading to continuous improvement and exponential growth.

How Micro-Adjustments Drive Massive Success

The Power of Small Changes

Most people believe that success comes from big, dramatic changes. However, true, lasting success is built through small, consistent adjustments over time. Micro-adjustments—tiny, deliberate shifts in behavior, mindset, or strategy—have the power to create massive results over weeks, months, and years.

The problem with grand overhauls is that they are difficult to sustain. Willpower fades, motivation fluctuates, and big changes often lead to burnout. Micro-adjustments, on the other hand, are subtle yet impactful—they allow you to course-correct with minimal effort while staying on track toward your goals.

This chapter explores how micro-adjustments in productivity, habits, mindset, and execution can exponentially improve results without overwhelming effort.

The Science Behind Micro-Adjustments

Micro-adjustments leverage a principle known as the compound effect, which states that small actions, repeated consistently, create exponential growth over time.

Why Micro-Adjustments Work:
- Low Resistance: Small changes are easier to implement than massive shifts.
- Compounding Growth: Tiny improvements accumulate, leading to big results.
- Sustained Momentum: Micro-adjustments keep progress steady without burnout.
- Increased Awareness: Small course corrections prevent major setbacks.

A 1% improvement each day might seem insignificant, but over a year, it results in a 37x improvement due to compounding. The key is consistency.

Micro-Adjustments in Productivity

High performance isn't about working harder—it's about working smarter. Making small tweaks to your workflow can dramatically improve efficiency and output.

1. Time Blocking Refinement

Instead of overhauling your entire schedule, start by adjusting one work block per day to focus on deep work. For example:

- Extend your highest-focus work session by 15 minutes.
- Reduce meeting durations by 10%.
- Schedule short mental resets between tasks to maintain focus.

2. Optimizing Your Workspace

Small changes in your environment can improve focus and productivity:

- Adjust your desk layout for better ergonomics.
- Place a distraction reminder (like a sticky note) on your monitor.
- Switch to a warmer or cooler light setting to improve concentration.

3. Incremental Email Adjustments

Email is a major time drain. Instead of a drastic approach, use micro-adjustments:

- Check email twice a day instead of five times.
- Unsubscribe from one irrelevant email list per day.
- Use templates for common responses to reduce typing time.

These tiny shifts streamline your workflow without overwhelming change.

Micro-Adjustments in Habits

The key to sustainable habit change is gradual progress, not radical transformation.

1. The 2-Minute Rule

Instead of committing to a massive new habit, start with just two minutes of action:

- Read one page of a book before bed.
- Do five push-ups instead of a full workout.
- Write one sentence instead of trying to complete a whole project.

Once the habit is started, it's much easier to keep going.

2. Slight Dietary Tweaks

Instead of a restrictive diet overhaul, make micro-adjustments:

- Drink one extra glass of water per day.
- Swap one sugary snack for a healthier option.
- Reduce portion sizes by 5% over time.

3. Gradual Sleep Improvements

Fixing sleep doesn't require a total routine overhaul:

- Go to bed 5 minutes earlier each night.
- Reduce screen time by 10% each day.
- Adjust wake-up time in small increments instead of all at once.

Micro-adjustments prevent overwhelm and make habit change effortless.

Micro-Adjustments in Mindset

Mindset shifts don't have to be dramatic. Tiny changes in thought patterns can rewire your brain for success over time.

1. The Language Shift

The words you use shape your mindset. Make small tweaks:

- Instead of "I have to," say "I get to."
- Instead of "I can't do this," say "I am learning to do this."
- Replace "I'm bad at this" with "I'm improving every day."

2. Daily Gratitude Adjustments

A slight shift in focus can change your emotional state:

- Write down one thing you're grateful for each morning.
- When frustrated, identify one positive aspect of the situation.

3. Reframing Setbacks

Instead of viewing failures as negative, tweak your perspective:

- Ask: "What lesson can I take from this?"
- Remind yourself: "Every mistake is part of growth."

These micro-adjustments build a resilient, success-driven mindset over time.

Micro-Adjustments in Execution

Execution is what separates dreamers from achievers. Making small, intentional refinements to how you execute can create massive long-term gains.

1. Refining Your Daily Priorities

Instead of listing 10+ tasks, micro-adjust your focus:

- Prioritize just three high-impact tasks per day.
- Reduce your to-do list by eliminating one unnecessary task daily.

2. Shortening Decision Loops

Overthinking kills execution. Make micro-adjustments to reduce decision time:

- Set a 90-second limit for small decisions.
- Use "if-then" rules: "If I receive a new task, then I immediately assign a deadline."

- Trust the first instinct on low-risk choices.

3. Breaking Large Goals into Micro-Wins

Big goals can feel overwhelming. Use micro-adjustments to create momentum:

- Break tasks into 5- to 10-minute mini-goals.
- Focus on completing one part at a time instead of aiming for perfection.
- Celebrate micro-wins to reinforce progress.

The Evening Review That Locks in Progress

The Power of Closing Your Day with Intention

The way you end your day is just as important as how you begin it. An effective evening review is a critical tool for sustained growth, productivity, and personal development. It allows you to reflect, refine, and prepare for the next day with clarity and purpose. Rather than letting days blend into one another, an intentional evening review helps you lock in progress and continuously improve.

Without an evening review, small mistakes compound, missed opportunities go unnoticed, and lessons fail to be absorbed. But when you take a few minutes each night to assess your wins, setbacks, and next steps, you create a cycle of continuous growth that leads to massive long-term success.

Why an Evening Review is Essential for Growth

A structured evening review does more than just provide a recap of your day—it solidifies learning, sharpens focus, and reinforces progress. Here's why it matters:

1. Reflection Strengthens Learning
    1.1. Without reflection, experiences lose value. Reviewing your day ensures you extract key lessons.
2. Reduces Mental Clutter
    2.1. Offloading thoughts onto paper clears your mind and improves sleep quality.
3. Builds Momentum for the Next Day
    3.1. Ending with clarity about tomorrow's priorities ensures you wake up ready to execute.
4. Creates Accountability
    4.1. Tracking progress increases self-awareness and eliminates excuses.
5. Enhances Emotional Resilience
    5.1. Recognizing small wins boosts motivation while identifying challenges fosters adaptability.

Step 1: Reflect on the Day's Wins and Lessons

Begin your evening review by assessing what went well and what could have been improved. Focus on insights rather than just listing events.

Questions to Ask:

- What were my biggest wins today?
- What progress did I make toward my goals?
- What worked well, and how can I replicate that success?
- What was my biggest challenge, and what can I learn from it?

The Gratitude Boost

Adding a gratitude component shifts your mindset toward positivity. Take a moment to write one thing you're grateful for that happened today—even if it was a small moment.

Step 2: Identify Sticking Points and Solutions

No day is perfect. The key to continuous growth is identifying obstacles and proactively seeking solutions.

Questions to Ask:

- What slowed me down or distracted me today?
- Did I face procrastination, and if so, why?
- What adjustments can I make to avoid these setbacks tomorrow?
- How did I handle stress, and what can I improve?

By addressing these sticking points, you prevent recurring problems and build a stronger execution framework over time.

Step 3: Review Key Metrics and Track Progress

What gets measured gets improved. Tracking small but consistent actions compounds into massive results.

Metrics to Track:

- Top 3 Priorities Completed – Did you achieve your most important tasks?
- Time Spent on High-Value Work – Were you productive or just busy?
- Energy Levels Throughout the Day – Did you work at peak performance?
- Daily Habit Streaks – Did you maintain consistency with important habits?

Use a simple journal, planner, or tracking app to log this data and observe trends over time.

Step 4: Plan the Next Day with Clarity

A strong evening review isn't just about looking back—it's about preparing for what's ahead. End each night with a clear plan for tomorrow so you wake up with purpose.

How to Plan Tomorrow Effectively:

- Define Your Top 1-3 Priorities
    - Identify the highest-impact tasks for the day.
- Time Block Your Focus Work
    - Assign specific hours for deep work sessions.
- Prepare Your Workspace

- Remove clutter, set up necessary materials, and ensure an efficient environment.
- Set a Personal Challenge
  - Add a small stretch goal to push yourself beyond routine tasks.

By doing this at night, you eliminate morning decision fatigue and start the next day already in motion.

Step 5: Implement a Wind-Down Routine for Rest and Recovery

Progress isn't just about execution—it's about sustaining high performance over time. Your evening routine should help signal to your brain that it's time to recharge so you can wake up refreshed and ready to perform.

Best Practices for an Effective Wind-Down Routine:

- Disconnect from Screens at Least 30 Minutes Before Bed
  - Blue light disrupts melatonin production and reduces sleep quality.
- Read or Listen to Something Inspiring
  - Choose personal development books, meditation, or reflective journaling.
- Engage in Light Stretching or Deep Breathing
  - Helps lower stress and relax the body before sleep.
- Reflect on Three Things You're Grateful For
  - Reinforces a positive mindset and reduces mental stress.

A structured wind-down routine ensures you end the day with clarity, focus, and peace of mind.

The Secret to Making Evening Reviews Stick

The power of the Evening Review isn't just in doing it once—it's in making it a consistent, automatic habit. Here's how to ensure it becomes part of your daily routine:

1. Set a Non-Negotiable Time

- Choose a specific time each night to conduct your review.
- Pair it with an existing habit (e.g., after brushing your teeth or before reading).

2. Keep It Simple and Sustainable

- Avoid making the process overwhelming—5-10 minutes is all it takes.
- Use a journal or a simple checklist to track insights.

3. Reflect, Adjust, and Repeat

- Over time, tweak your questions and process to fit your needs.
- Treat the evening review as an evolving system for self-improvement.

Summary: The Execution

Turning Plans into Daily Success

Having a great strategy and ambitious goals means nothing without execution. Part 3: The Execution focuses on the systems, habits, and mindset shifts needed to consistently take action and make meaningful progress. This section is about turning plans into reality through structured daily routines, overcoming resistance, and optimizing performance with reflection and micro-adjustments.

Designing a Winning Day

Success starts with structuring your day for productivity and impact. The key is intentional planning, breaking tasks into manageable action blocks, and focusing on the highest-value work instead of just being busy. The Topify Productivity Planner provides a framework for ensuring that every day moves you closer to your goals.

The key principles include:

- Starting with a strong morning mindset to set the tone for execution.
- Using structured action blocks to work deeply without distractions.
- Distinguishing between busy work and productive work to ensure efforts are aligned with meaningful outcomes.

Overcoming Resistance and Taking Action

Procrastination and hesitation are the biggest killers of progress. This section explores the psychology of procrastination—why we delay important work and how to overcome it. Instead of relying on motivation, the focus is on rewiring the brain for execution through discipline and structured habits.

Key takeaways include:

- Understanding that resistance is normal and must be faced, not avoided.
- Using habit-stacking, accountability systems, and micro-commitments to break inertia.
- Winning even when motivation fails by relying on processes instead of emotions.

The 45-Second Reset and Continuous Refinement

Execution isn't about perfection; it's about course correction. The 45-Second Reset is a simple but powerful tool that allows for instant recalibration when focus drifts. Rather than letting setbacks derail momentum, small adjustments keep progress on track.

Supporting this idea, the Topify Reflection Method ensures that daily, weekly, and monthly insights are captured, analyzed, and refined. Instead of repeating mistakes, this process allows for continuous learning, optimizing, and fine-tuning of personal performance.

Locking in Progress with the Evening Review

The day isn't complete without an intentional review process. By reflecting on wins, challenges, and key lessons, progress is reinforced, and clarity is created for the next day. The Evening Review strengthens execution by:

- Recognizing accomplishments and reinforcing positive habits.
- Identifying obstacles and creating immediate course corrections.
- Preparing for the next day so execution starts without hesitation.

Part 4: The Scaling Effect

Executing consistently is the foundation of success, but scaling that success requires a different approach. Many people plateau once they achieve a certain level of progress, unable to break through to the next level. What separates those who continue to grow and achieve extraordinary results is their ability to focus deeply, leverage external support, and adopt the mindset of elite performers.

The Scaling Effect is about amplifying your impact. It's not just about working harder—it's about working smarter, more effectively, and in alignment with the habits of high achievers. This part of the book explores the strategies that allow you to break free from limitations, remove distractions, and build a sustainable system for continued growth and peak performance.

What You'll Discover in This Section:

- Chapter 9: Mastering Focus in a Distracted World – The modern world is designed to pull your attention in a thousand directions. This chapter will teach you how to eliminate digital and mental clutter, create deep work environments, and develop the art of saying no without guilt, ensuring you stay focused on what truly matters.
- Chapter 10: Leveraging Accountability & Feedback – Self-discipline alone won't take you to the highest levels of success. Here, you'll learn why external accountability is the missing piece in execution. You'll discover how to build a Topify Circle of accountability, use public and

private commitments to stay on track, and integrate continuous feedback loops for improvement.
- Chapter 11: Thinking Like a High Performer – The best performers in any field don't just work harder—they think differently. This chapter breaks down the key mindset shifts that separate average execution from elite performance. You'll learn how to embrace discomfort, operate at a higher level, and unlock the mental frameworks used by world-class achievers.

By the end of this section, you'll have a scalable system for success—one that ensures you don't just achieve your goals but continue to elevate and expand them over time. Let's dive into the advanced strategies that will help you scale your focus, execution, and results to the highest level.

Chapter 9: Mastering Focus in a Distracted World

We live in an age of constant distraction. From endless notifications to the ever-present pull of social media, the modern world is designed to steal your focus and attention. If you don't take control of your focus, someone else will. The ability to concentrate deeply on meaningful work is now one of the most valuable skills you can develop.

In a world where attention spans are shrinking, those who can sustain deep focus will rise above the noise and accomplish far more in less time. Yet, mastering focus is not about working harder—it's about removing distractions, creating the right environments, and learning how to direct your attention with intention.

This chapter will explore how to eliminate digital and mental clutter, establish deep work habits, and master the art of saying no without guilt. True productivity isn't about doing more; it's about doing what matters most with complete focus.

What You'll Learn in This Chapter:

- How digital distractions hijack your brain and how to reclaim control
- The science behind deep work and how to train your focus like a muscle
- How to create an environment that enhances, rather than diminishes, concentration

- Why saying no is a superpower and how to set firm boundaries without guilt

By the end of this chapter, you'll have a system for protecting your attention, eliminating distractions, and maximizing deep work, ensuring that every minute spent working moves you closer to success.

Eliminating Digital and Mental Clutter

The Hidden Cost of Clutter

Clutter—both digital and mental—is one of the greatest obstacles to deep focus and productivity. It creates unnecessary noise, reduces cognitive capacity, and leads to stress, decision fatigue, and inaction. In today's fast-paced world, information overload and constant digital distractions are the new normal, making it harder than ever to concentrate on meaningful work. To reclaim focus, we must learn to eliminate digital distractions and declutter our minds.

By reducing digital noise and simplifying mental processes, you free up valuable cognitive resources that can be directed toward high-impact work and better decision-making. This chapter will provide actionable strategies to cut through the clutter, organize your digital and mental space, and regain control over your attention.

Part 1: Digital Clutter – The Silent Productivity Killer

Digital clutter is a hidden productivity drain. Emails, notifications, open tabs, and excessive screen time fragment your attention and make deep focus nearly impossible. Your devices should work for you—not against you.

1. Decluttering Your Digital Workspace

- Inbox Zero Strategy: Reduce email overload by implementing filters, unsubscribing from unnecessary newsletters, and setting specific times to check your inbox.
- Organized File System: Create a structured folder system for quick file retrieval instead of wasting time searching for documents.
- Limiting Open Tabs: Keep only essential tabs open; use tools like tab managers to reduce screen clutter.

2. Taking Control of Notifications

- Turn Off Non-Essential Notifications: Social media, email, and app alerts are designed to hijack your attention.
- Use "Do Not Disturb" Mode: Schedule focused work blocks where all non-essential notifications are silenced.
- Batch Communication: Set dedicated times for emails and messages instead of responding throughout the day.

3. Reducing Screen Time

- Implement the 2-Hour Rule: Limit non-work-related screen use to two hours per day.
- Use Website Blockers: Tools like Freedom or Cold Turkey can help limit time on distracting sites.
- Create Device-Free Zones: Establish areas (e.g., bedroom, dining table) where no screens are allowed.

Part 2: Mental Clutter – The Mind's Constant Noise

Mental clutter is just as disruptive as digital clutter. Racing thoughts, excessive to-do lists, and overcommitments lead to overwhelm and decision fatigue. A clear mind is a productive mind.

1. Practicing Thought Decluttering

- Morning Brain Dump: Spend 5 minutes writing down everything on your mind to clear mental space.
- Journaling for Clarity: Reflect on priorities and declutter intrusive thoughts.
- Single-Tasking Over Multitasking: Focus on one task at a time to reduce mental overload.

2. Simplifying Decision-Making

- Eliminate Minor Choices: Automate routine decisions (e.g., meal planning, outfit selection) to conserve mental energy.

- Use the Two-Minute Rule: If something takes less than two minutes, do it immediately.
- Limit Daily To-Dos: Stick to a Top 3 Priorities approach rather than overwhelming yourself with long lists.

3. Creating Space for Deep Work

- Set Boundaries: Protect deep work sessions by communicating them clearly to others.
- Incorporate Mindfulness Techniques: Meditation, deep breathing, and short breaks can reset focus.
- Optimize Your Work Environment: Declutter your workspace to remove physical distractions.

How to Create Deep Work Environments

The Importance of Deep Work

In an age of distractions, the ability to engage in deep work—uninterrupted, focused effort on meaningful tasks—has become a rare and powerful skill. Deep work isn't just about working hard; it's about creating an environment that allows you to think clearly, stay engaged, and produce high-quality results.

Without a proper deep work environment, distractions continuously pull us away from meaningful progress. Every notification, background noise, and open tab weakens our ability to focus deeply. By intentionally designing a workspace and routine that fosters deep work, you can significantly increase productivity, creativity, and overall effectiveness.

This chapter will provide practical strategies to eliminate distractions, optimize your workspace, and develop habits that support deep, meaningful work.

Step 1: Eliminate External Distractions

The first step to creating a deep work environment is removing external distractions that pull attention away from high-priority tasks.

1. Declutter Your Physical Workspace

- Keep only essential items on your desk (laptop, notebook, water, and relevant materials).
- Remove visual clutter—a messy desk can increase cognitive load and stress.
- Optimize lighting to reduce eye strain and enhance focus.

2. Control Noise and Interruptions

- Use noise-canceling headphones or play non-distracting background sounds (white noise, instrumental music).
- Set clear boundaries with colleagues or family members about deep work time.
- Consider a "Do Not Disturb" sign or closed-door policy to minimize interruptions.

3. Manage Digital Distractions

- Turn off notifications on your phone and computer.
- Use website blockers (Freedom, Cold Turkey, or FocusMe) to prevent social media and email distractions.
- Work in full-screen mode to avoid unnecessary multitasking.

By reducing these distractions, you create an environment where focus comes naturally rather than being a constant battle.

Step 2: Optimize Your Work Environment for Deep Focus

A well-designed workspace supports mental clarity and deep concentration. Even small environmental changes can significantly impact productivity.

1. Lighting and Air Quality

- Use natural light or a daylight lamp to enhance alertness and mood.
- Keep air circulation fresh—poor air quality reduces cognitive performance.
- Add plants to your workspace to improve air quality and reduce stress.

2. Ergonomics and Comfort

- Use an ergonomic chair and desk to prevent discomfort and fatigue.
- Maintain a neutral posture with your screen at eye level.

- Take micro-breaks every hour to stretch and prevent strain.

3. Designate a Deep Work Zone

- Have a dedicated area for deep work separate from casual activities.
- If working remotely, use a specific chair or desk for work only.
- Avoid working from your bed or couch, as this weakens mental associations with focus.

A well-structured environment reduces friction between you and deep work, making it easier to enter a flow state.

Step 3: Implement Time Strategies for Deep Work

Your environment isn't just physical—it's also how you structure your time. Deep work is most effective when scheduled and protected.

1. Use Time Blocking

- Schedule deep work in 90-minute blocks, followed by short breaks.
- Align deep work with your peak energy hours (morning for most people).
- Treat deep work blocks as unbreakable appointments with yourself.

2. The Pomodoro Technique for Focused Sprints

- Work for 25-45 minutes, then take a 5-minute break.
- Use a countdown timer to create urgency and sustain concentration.
- After four deep work sessions, take a longer break (15-30 minutes).

3. Themed Workdays for Greater Efficiency

- Dedicate specific days or hours to deep work vs. administrative tasks.
- Example: Monday-Wednesday for deep work, Thursday-Friday for meetings and admin.
- Prevents constant task-switching, which kills focus and efficiency.

Step 4: Train Your Brain for Deep Focus

A deep work environment is only effective if your mind is conditioned to focus. Developing mental discipline ensures you stay engaged and avoid distractions.

1. Develop a Pre-Work Ritual

- Start each session with a ritual (meditation, stretching, setting an intention).
- Helps signal to your brain that it's time to focus.
- Reduces resistance to getting started.

2. Build Focus Stamina

- Start with short deep work sessions (30 minutes) and gradually increase.
- Over time, train your brain to sustain longer periods of intense focus.

3. Use Visualization for Concentration

- Before starting deep work, visualize yourself completing the task.
- This technique increases commitment and reduces distractions.

Deep focus is like a muscle—the more you train it, the stronger it becomes.

Step 5: Evaluate and Refine Your Deep Work Practices

Creating a deep work environment isn't a one-time event—it's a continuous process of refining what works best for you.

1. Track Your Focus Sessions

- Keep a log of how long you focus before distractions arise.
- Identify patterns of peak performance and align deep work accordingly.
- Adjust strategies based on what improves your results.

2. Conduct Weekly Reflection
- Ask: What worked well in my deep work sessions?
- Adjust your environment, schedule, and mindset based on insights.
- Commit to one small improvement per week to maintain growth.

By consistently refining your deep work environment, you ensure that focus becomes a natural and sustainable part of your workflow.

The Art of Saying No Without Guilt

Why Saying No is Essential

Most people struggle to say no. They fear disappointing others, missing out on opportunities, or being perceived as unhelpful. However, saying yes to everything spreads you too thin, drains your energy, and prevents you from focusing on what truly matters.

Mastering the art of saying no is not about rejecting people or being selfish—it's about protecting your time, energy, and priorities. Those who achieve the highest levels of success do so because they are selective about where they invest their time. By learning to say no without guilt, you take control of your life and work toward your goals with greater clarity and efficiency.

Step 1: Understand Why Saying No Feels Difficult

Saying no triggers emotional discomfort because it often comes with social and psychological pressures. Here's why people struggle:

1. Fear of Disappointing Others – You don't want to let people down.
2. Desire to Be Liked – You associate saying yes with approval and acceptance.
3. Guilt from Prior Commitments – You feel obligated to return favors.
4. FOMO (Fear of Missing Out) – You worry about losing opportunities.
5. Cultural or Upbringing Influence – Many were raised to believe saying no is rude or unkind.

By recognizing these patterns, you can begin to shift your mindset and see saying no as a positive act that protects your well-being.

Step 2: Shift Your Mindset – No is a Boundary, Not a Rejection

Instead of viewing no as a rejection, reframe it as a boundary-setting tool that allows you to prioritize what truly matters.

- Saying no to distractions means saying yes to your priorities.
- Setting boundaries is a sign of self-respect, not selfishness.

- People respect those who are clear about their time and commitments.

When you say no, you are choosing to protect your mental space, energy, and goals. The most successful people understand that every yes must be earned.

Step 3: Strategies for Saying No Gracefully

Saying no doesn't have to be harsh or awkward. Use these techniques to decline requests politely and assertively.

1. The Direct No (For Clear and Firm Boundaries)

- *Example:* "I appreciate the offer, but I have to decline."
- Works best when you need to be straightforward and leave no room for negotiation.

2. The Soft No with an Alternative

- *Example:* "I can't commit to this, but I'd be happy to help in a smaller way."
- Provides a middle ground when you don't want to say yes but still want to contribute.

3. The Delayed Response

- *Example:* "Let me check my schedule and get back to you."
- Gives you time to consider if the request aligns with your priorities before deciding.

4. The Referral No

- *Example:* "I'm not available, but I can recommend someone else who might help."
- Redirects the request while still providing value.

5. The Priority-Based No

- *Example:* "I'm focusing on [specific priority] right now, so I won't be able to take this on."
- Reinforces that your no is about priorities, not rejection.

Step 4: Setting Personal and Professional Boundaries

To avoid the need for constant decision-making about requests, establish clear boundaries ahead of time.

1. Define Your Non-Negotiables – Identify the commitments you will always prioritize.
2. Create Standard Responses – Prepare polite but firm phrases to use when declining requests.
3. Limit Access – Set boundaries around when and how people can reach you.
4. Respect Your Own Time – Treat your time as valuable as you would for others.

Setting these boundaries in advance makes it easier to say no without guilt or hesitation.

Step 5: Overcoming Guilt and Fear

If saying no makes you feel guilty, remind yourself:

- Your time and energy are limited resources. Protecting them isn't selfish.
- People who respect you will understand your boundaries.
- Every yes to the wrong thing is a no to the right thing.
- Successful people say no often and without guilt.

With practice, saying no becomes second nature, and you'll feel more in control of your decisions and commitments.

Chapter 10: Leveraging Accountability & Feedback

Success is rarely a solo effort. The world's highest achievers—whether in business, sports, or personal development—understand the immense power of accountability and feedback. While self-discipline is crucial, external structures ensure that progress remains consistent, challenges are addressed in real-time, and goals are met with greater efficiency.

Most people set goals with good intentions but struggle with execution. Without accountability, motivation fluctuates, priorities shift, and setbacks feel insurmountable. Similarly, without feedback, it's easy to repeat mistakes or stagnate without realizing it. This chapter explores why accountability isn't just a motivational tool—it's a performance multiplier.

Why Accountability and Feedback Matter

1. Accountability Eliminates Excuses – When you answer to someone else, you are far less likely to procrastinate or give up.
2. Feedback Provides Clarity – Honest, constructive feedback helps refine strategies and improves execution.
3. External Pressure Creates Internal Drive – When others expect progress from you, you naturally perform at a higher level.

4. Progress is Measured, Not Assumed – Regular check-ins ensure that small improvements compound over time.

What You'll Learn in This Chapter

- Why self-discipline alone isn't enough and how accountability changes the game.
- How to build a Topify Circle of accountability—a network of people who push you to stay on track.
- The difference between public and private commitments, and when to use each.
- How to receive and implement feedback effectively without feeling defensive.

By the end of this chapter, you'll have a system that keeps you committed, ensures steady progress, and turns feedback into an advantage rather than a source of stress.

Why Self-Discipline Isn't Enough

The Myth of Self-Discipline

Self-discipline is often glorified as the key to success. The idea that sheer willpower alone can drive us to achieve our biggest goals is both appealing and misleading. While discipline plays an important role in execution, it is not a limitless resource, and relying solely on it leads to exhaustion, inconsistency, and failure.

The reality? Discipline is a starting point, not a complete system for success. The highest achievers in the world don't operate on willpower alone—they leverage accountability, structure, and external feedback to sustain long-term progress. This chapter explores why self-discipline has limitations and how to create systems that ensure success, even when willpower runs low.

The Limits of Self-Discipline

Self-discipline is a valuable tool, but it has three fundamental flaws:

1. Discipline Fades Over Time

- Willpower is like a muscle—it fatigues with use. The more decisions you make in a day, the weaker your self-control becomes.
- Studies show that decision fatigue leads to poor choices, procrastination, and impulse-driven actions.
- Example: Someone starting a fitness journey might rely on discipline to hit the gym daily, but as motivation wanes, skipping workouts becomes easier unless external structures are in place.

2. Emotions Disrupt Discipline

- On high-energy, motivated days, discipline is easier. But what happens when stress, fatigue, or unexpected obstacles arise?

- Without external accountability, it's easy to justify skipping tasks, procrastinating, or shifting priorities.
- Example: A writer may plan to write 1,000 words per day, but if a stressful event occurs, the plan collapses without external reinforcement.

3. Discipline Without Strategy is Ineffective

- Many people equate discipline with working harder rather than working smarter.
- Simply forcing yourself to "stay disciplined" without a clear, structured plan leads to wasted effort and burnout.
- Example: Someone trying to grow a business may work 12-hour days without prioritizing high-impact activities, leading to exhaustion rather than success.

The Role of External Accountability

If discipline alone isn't enough, what ensures consistency and execution? Accountability.

1. Accountability Eliminates Excuses

- When you commit to someone else, you create external pressure to follow through.
- Public commitments increase the likelihood of success because they tap into our desire to be seen as reliable.

2. Feedback Accelerates Growth

- Without feedback, you may unknowingly repeat ineffective behaviors.
- An outside perspective helps refine strategies and improve efficiency.

3. Accountability Creates Momentum

- When progress is tracked and reviewed, small wins build confidence and reinforce positive habits.
- Weekly check-ins with an accountability partner prevent stagnation and keep motivation high.

The Power of Systems Over Discipline

Instead of relying on sheer willpower, successful people build systems that remove the need for constant discipline. Here's how:

1. Automate Key Decisions

- Reduce decision fatigue by pre-planning meals, workouts, or work blocks.
- Use scheduling tools and reminders to eliminate daily choice-making.

2. Leverage Social Accountability

- Join masterminds, coaching programs, or peer groups to ensure progress.
- Use an accountability partner to stay on track with key goals.

3. Create Rituals and Triggers

- Design cues that prompt desired behaviors automatically.
- Example: Setting out workout clothes the night before makes morning exercise more likely.

Building a Topify Circle of Accountability

Why Accountability Drives Success

Success isn't just about effort and discipline—it's about consistency, and the best way to maintain consistency is through accountability. When left to our own devices, it's easy to let distractions, procrastination, or self-doubt derail our progress. This is why some of the world's highest achievers, from elite athletes to top entrepreneurs, rely on accountability circles to push them toward their goals.

The Topify Circle of Accountability is a structured way to create a personal or professional network that holds you to your commitments, provides feedback, and ensures you stay on track. Instead of working in isolation, you surround yourself with people who challenge, support, and propel you toward success.

Step 1: Understanding the Power of an Accountability Circle

A Topify Circle is a small group of individuals who commit to holding each other accountable for their goals. This creates an environment of support, challenge, and growth, making it far easier to follow through on commitments.

Benefits of an Accountability Circle:

- Eliminates excuses – Others won't let you slide on your commitments.
- Increases motivation – Seeing others progress inspires action.
- Provides feedback – Honest insights help refine your approach.
- Boosts consistency – Regular check-ins prevent slumps.
- Creates external pressure – You're more likely to follow through when others are watching.

Without accountability, it's easy to let goals slip, but a Topify Circle ensures constant forward movement.

Step 2: Choosing the Right People for Your Circle

Your accountability circle is only as strong as the people within it. The right group will elevate your performance, while the wrong group can lead to stagnation.

Ideal Characteristics of Accountability Partners:

1. Committed – They take their goals as seriously as you do.

2. Supportive but Honest – They provide encouragement but also tough love.
3. Goal-Oriented – They have their own targets and understand the value of accountability.
4. Trustworthy – Open communication is essential for success.
5. Diverse Perspectives – Different experiences provide valuable insights.

Who Should You Avoid?

- Chronic excuse-makers – They will drag down the group's energy.
- Overly negative people – Constructive criticism is great, but constant pessimism is toxic.
- Those who don't follow through – An accountability circle only works if everyone is committed.

Step 3: Structuring Your Accountability Circle

A strong accountability circle needs structure to be effective. Without clear guidelines, it can turn into a casual chat group rather than a results-driven team.

Key Elements of a Topify Circle:

1. Regular Check-ins – Weekly or bi-weekly meetings to review progress.
2. Goal Setting Sessions – Each member sets and shares clear, measurable goals.

3. Progress Tracking – Use shared documents, apps, or spreadsheets to monitor progress.
4. Feedback Loops – Provide constructive feedback to help each other improve.
5. Commitment Rules – Each member agrees to uphold the circle's values and commitments.

By formalizing the group's structure, you create accountability momentum that leads to long-term success.

Step 4: Running Effective Accountability Meetings

Meetings should be focused and action-driven. To prevent wasted time, stick to a structured format.

Suggested Meeting Agenda:

1. Wins & Progress Updates (10 minutes)
   - Each member shares key achievements since the last meeting.
1. Challenges & Obstacles (15 minutes)
   - Discuss roadblocks and get input from the group on solutions.
1. Commitments for the Next Session (10 minutes)
   - Set specific, actionable goals before the next meeting.
1. Feedback Round (10 minutes)
   - Members offer constructive feedback to help refine strategies.
1. Final Thoughts & Motivation Boost (5 minutes)

- Close the meeting on a high note with encouragement and motivation.

Having a set structure ensures meetings remain productive, efficient, and results-oriented.

Step 5: Leveraging Public and Private Commitments

Accountability is most effective when commitments are made both privately and publicly.

Private Accountability (Within the Group):

- Sharing goals with your Topify Circle creates personal responsibility.
- Members regularly check in to track progress and provide support.

Public Accountability:

- Announcing key goals publicly (social media, a blog, or a community) creates external pressure to follow through.
- Public commitments increase the likelihood of success because they tap into our psychological need to remain consistent with what we say.

Using both forms of accountability ensures you stay on course and maintain high levels of commitment.

Step 6: Adapting and Evolving the Circle Over Time

Your Topify Circle should grow and evolve as you progress. Regularly evaluate what's working and what needs improvement.

Ways to Strengthen Your Accountability Circle:

1. Evaluate the group's effectiveness every 3-6 months.
2. Encourage deeper challenges – Push each other to go beyond comfort zones.
3. Celebrate wins publicly – Recognize and reward achievements.
4. Rotate leadership roles – Different members can lead meetings for variety.
5. Invite new, high-performing members – Fresh energy keeps the group dynamic.

A well-maintained accountability circle doesn't just maintain progress—it accelerates it.

The Power of Public and Private Commitments

Why Commitment is the Key to Success

The difference between setting a goal and achieving it often comes down to commitment. Making a commitment—whether to yourself or to others—creates a powerful psychological force that drives action, builds momentum, and eliminates hesitation. However, not all commitments are the same. The way you structure them can determine whether they help or hinder your progress.

The two most effective forms of commitment are public and private commitments. Both play unique roles in motivation, accountability, and long-term success. Understanding how to leverage them effectively ensures that your goals don't remain mere aspirations but translate into real, measurable progress.

The Psychology of Commitment

Commitment taps into two fundamental psychological principles:

1. The Consistency Principle – Humans have an innate desire to act in alignment with what they've publicly stated or privately decided.
2. Social Accountability – When others expect us to follow through, we feel increased pressure to stay true to our word.

By utilizing both public and private commitments, you create a dual accountability system that keeps you aligned with your goals, even when motivation wavers.

Public Commitments: The Power of External Accountability

A public commitment is when you share your goal or intention with others—friends, family, colleagues, or even the public via social media. This external declaration increases the likelihood of follow-through.

Benefits of Public Commitments:

- Increases Accountability: When others are aware of your goals, you're less likely to abandon them.
- Boosts Motivation: Social pressure can be a powerful motivator when discipline fades.
- Creates Support Networks: Publicly stating a goal can attract like-minded individuals who provide encouragement, advice, or collaboration opportunities.
- Enhances Performance: Studies show that those who make their goals public tend to achieve them more consistently.

Best Practices for Public Commitments:

- Be Specific: Instead of saying, "I want to get fit," say, "I will go to the gym 3 times a week for the next 3 months."
- Choose the Right Audience: Share commitments with people who will genuinely support and encourage you.
- Track and Share Progress: Regular updates reinforce the commitment and inspire others.
- Use Public Challenges: Engaging in a social challenge (e.g., a 30-day challenge) can amplify accountability.

Private Commitments: The Strength of Internal Discipline

A private commitment is a personal agreement you make with yourself, often without announcing it to others. This type of commitment strengthens internal motivation and self-discipline.

Benefits of Private Commitments:

- Eliminates External Pressure: Reduces fear of judgment or external expectations.
- Builds Self-Reliance: Develops personal discipline and self-accountability.
- Encourages Deeper Reflection: Allows you to pursue goals that are personally meaningful rather than socially influenced.
- Provides Flexibility: Enables goal adjustments without external scrutiny.

Best Practices for Private Commitments:

- Write It Down: Physically documenting goals increases the likelihood of achieving them.
- Create Personal Milestones: Break big goals into smaller, measurable steps.
- Use a Habit Tracker: Tracking progress reinforces consistency.
- Develop Self-Check-Ins: Set a weekly time to review progress and make necessary adjustments.

How to Combine Public and Private Commitments for Maximum Impact

The most effective strategy is a hybrid approach—leveraging both public and private commitments in a way that maximizes their strengths while minimizing their weaknesses.

1. Start with a Private Commitment

    - Define your goal clearly before sharing it with others.
    - Ensure it aligns with your values and long-term aspirations.
    - Take initial action privately to build confidence before announcing it publicly.

2. Use Public Commitment for High-Stakes Goals

    - Announce major goals where social accountability will push you to follow through.
    - Engage in public tracking (social media updates, blog posts, challenge groups).
    - Surround yourself with a strong support system that holds you to your word.

3. Keep Some Goals Private for Personal Growth

    - If a goal is deeply personal or experimental, consider keeping it private until you build momentum.
    - Use internal accountability methods like journaling and progress tracking.
    - Prioritize self-discipline as a foundational skill.

Common Pitfalls and How to Avoid Them

While commitments are powerful, they can backfire if not managed correctly.

1. Overcommitting Publicly

   - Problem: Declaring too many goals at once can lead to overwhelm and failure.
   - Solution: Focus on one or two key public commitments at a time.

2. Relying Too Much on External Validation

   - Problem: If public praise becomes the primary motivation, intrinsic motivation may weaken.
   - Solution: Balance public commitments with private, deeply personal goals.

3. Lack of Follow-Through

   - Problem: Making public commitments but failing to take action damages credibility.
   - Solution: Set realistic goals and ensure a structured follow-up plan.

Chapter 11: Thinking Like a High Performer

What separates high performers from the rest? It's not just talent, intelligence, or luck—it's how they think. High performers have a fundamentally different approach to challenges, productivity, and success. They prioritize execution over excuses, embrace discomfort as a tool for growth, and consistently push beyond average limits.

In a world filled with distractions, most people operate on autopilot, reacting to their environment instead of taking intentional control. High performers, on the other hand, have a strategic mindset that allows them to break through limitations and consistently operate at their best. They don't wait for motivation; they create systems that ensure results. They don't fear failure; they see it as feedback.

This chapter explores the core mental frameworks and habits that define elite achievers. You'll learn how to shift your thinking, develop resilience, and adopt the mindset of a top performer. By the end, you'll have a clear roadmap to elevate your thought processes, make better decisions, and execute at a higher level.

What You'll Learn in This Chapter

- The key differences between average and elite execution
- How to retrain your brain for success and consistency
- The power of embracing discomfort and using it as fuel for growth

- Practical strategies to adopt a high-performance mindset and apply it daily

Success isn't reserved for a select few—it's the result of intentional thought patterns and habits. This chapter will show you how to cultivate the mental edge that drives sustained excellence.

The Difference Between Average and Elite Execution

Why Execution Separates the Best from the Rest

Many people set goals, but only a small percentage truly achieve elite-level results. The difference between average and high performers isn't talent, luck, or intelligence—it's execution. How you take action, follow through, and refine your approach determines whether you stay stuck in mediocrity or rise to the top.

Average execution is reactive, inconsistent, and effort-driven. Elite execution, on the other hand, is strategic, consistent, and outcome-driven. High performers don't just work harder—they work smarter, with greater clarity and precision. This chapter breaks down the key differences between average execution and elite execution, providing actionable steps to elevate your performance to the highest level.

1. Clarity vs. Confusion: Knowing Exactly What to Do

Average Execution:

- Works on too many tasks at once without a clear focus.
- Prioritizes busywork over high-impact actions.
- Lacks clarity on long-term objectives, leading to wasted effort.

Elite Execution:

- Focuses only on high-leverage activities that drive the biggest results.
- Sets clear, measurable goals and reverse-engineers the process to achieve them.
- Eliminates distractions and unnecessary commitments to maximize efficiency.

How to Apply This:

- Define your Top 3 Priorities every day.
- Use The 80/20 Rule (Pareto Principle) to focus on the 20% of actions that generate 80% of results.
- Cut unnecessary meetings, commitments, and low-value tasks.

2. Proactive vs. Reactive Work

Average Execution:

- Waits for problems to arise before taking action.

- Spends the day responding to emails, notifications, and other people's priorities.
- Gets caught in a cycle of putting out fires instead of making progress.

Elite Execution:

- Starts the day with a clear plan, attacking the most important tasks first.
- Prepares for challenges in advance and minimizes disruptions.
- Builds systems that automate or eliminate low-value tasks to free up mental energy.

How to Apply This:

- Time block your most important work before checking emails or messages.
- Identify recurring problems and build preventative systems.
- Set clear boundaries—don't let other people's urgencies derail your priorities.

3. Consistency vs. Motivation-Driven Work

Average Execution:

- Works hard only when motivated.
- Struggles with consistency, leading to unpredictable results.

- Abandons routines when things get difficult or inconvenient.

Elite Execution:

- Shows up and executes regardless of motivation.
- Has non-negotiable daily habits that drive long-term success.
- Knows that discipline beats motivation every time.

How to Apply This:

- Implement The 2-Day Rule: Never skip your habits two days in a row.
- Create pre-commitments (e.g., book workouts in advance, schedule deep work sessions).
- Set up accountability systems to stay consistent even when motivation dips.

4. Speed of Execution vs. Overthinking

Average Execution:

- Spends too much time researching, planning, and second-guessing.
- Waits for perfect conditions before taking action.
- Suffers from analysis paralysis, leading to delays and inaction.

Elite Execution:

- Acts quickly and adjusts along the way.
- Understands that imperfect action beats perfect inaction.
- Learns from experience rather than excessive planning.

How to Apply This:

- Follow the 70% Rule: If you have 70% of the information, execute and refine later.
- Set decision deadlines to prevent overthinking.
- Remember: Action creates momentum—waiting kills it.

5. Resilience vs. Giving Up Too Soon

Average Execution:

- Gives up after encountering obstacles or failures.
- Takes failure personally and avoids risk.
- Lacks mental toughness to push through discomfort.

Elite Execution:

- Sees failure as data, not defeat.
- Adapts quickly and adjusts the approach instead of quitting.
- Pushes through setbacks with a long-term mindset.

How to Apply This:

- Reframe failure: Ask "What did this teach me?" instead of "Why did I fail?"

- Use The 45-Second Reset: When something goes wrong, take 45 seconds to reset and refocus.
- Develop mental resilience through challenges rather than avoiding them.

6. Feedback vs. Operating in Isolation

Average Execution:

- Avoids feedback due to fear of criticism.
- Works in isolation without external accountability.
- Gets stuck in old patterns due to lack of outside perspective.

Elite Execution:

- Actively seeks feedback to refine execution.
- Uses accountability partners, mentors, or peer groups for guidance.
- Views constructive criticism as a tool for improvement, not a personal attack.

How to Apply This:

- Join an accountability group or hire a coach.
- Request specific feedback (e.g., "How can I improve X?") instead of vague advice.
- Implement one improvement per week based on feedback.

Choose to Execute at an Elite Level

Execution is the ultimate differentiator between those who dream and those who achieve. The difference between average and elite execution isn't talent or intelligence—it's about:

- Clarity over confusion.
- Proactive work over reactive work.
- Consistency over motivation.
- Speed over perfectionism.
- Resilience over quitting.
- Feedback-driven growth over working in isolation.

By shifting your execution approach from average to elite, you separate yourself from 99% of people who merely set goals. Excellence isn't reserved for the few—it's available to those who commit to executing at the highest level.

Now, the choice is yours: Will you settle for average execution, or will you step up and execute like an elite performer? Adopting the Mindset of World-Class Achievers

The Mindset That Defines Excellence

Success is rarely an accident. The world's highest achievers, whether in business, sports, or personal development, don't just work harder than others—they think differently. Their mindset is built on a foundation of resilience, clarity, and an unshakable commitment to excellence.

Adopting a world-class mindset isn't about innate talent or luck; it's about cultivating mental frameworks and habits that drive elite-level success. By shifting how you approach challenges, decision-making, and growth, you can unlock new levels of performance and execution.

This chapter explores the core beliefs, thought patterns, and strategies that define world-class achievers—and how you can integrate them into your own life.

1. Thinking Big: Expanding Your Vision

Average Performers:

- Set goals that feel safe and realistic.
- Stay within their comfort zone, avoiding risks.
- View limitations as barriers to success.

World-Class Achievers:

- Set audacious, bold goals that challenge their potential.
- See obstacles as stepping stones rather than roadblocks.
- Believe that growth happens through pushing limits.

How to Apply This:

- Use vision-setting exercises to expand your perspective.
- Ask yourself: *What would I attempt if I knew I couldn't fail?*
- Surround yourself with people who think bigger than you do.

2. The Power of Relentless Execution

Average Performers:

- Start projects but struggle to follow through.
- Wait for motivation before taking action.
- Get discouraged by slow progress.

World-Class Achievers:

- Commit to execution regardless of mood or motivation.
- Build habits that reinforce discipline and consistency.
- Focus on continuous progress over perfection.

How to Apply This:

- Implement the 2-Minute Rule: Start tasks immediately, even if small.
- Develop a daily action plan that prioritizes key objectives.
- Celebrate small wins to build momentum and confidence.

3. Resilience and Adaptability: Thriving Under Pressure

Average Performers:

- Let setbacks derail their confidence and motivation.
- Avoid discomfort and give up when things get tough.
- Struggle to adapt when faced with unexpected challenges.

World-Class Achievers:

- View failure as a necessary part of growth.
- Develop a growth mindset, seeing challenges as opportunities to improve.
- Adjust strategies quickly rather than dwelling on setbacks.

How to Apply This:

- Reframe failure: Ask *What lesson did this teach me?*
- Develop stress-management techniques to stay composed under pressure.
- Use adaptive problem-solving to find alternative solutions.

4. Extreme Ownership and Accountability

Average Performers:

- Blame external circumstances for lack of success.
- Avoid responsibility for mistakes and failures.
- Struggle to take decisive action.

World-Class Achievers:

- Take full ownership of their results—good or bad.
- Learn from failures rather than making excuses.
- Seek feedback proactively and apply it constructively.

How to Apply This:

- Develop a habit of self-reflection to assess performance honestly.
- Hold yourself accountable through public or peer commitments.
- Focus on solutions, not excuses.

5. The Obsession with Growth and Learning

Average Performers:

- Stick to what they already know and resist new ideas.
- Let ego prevent them from seeking mentorship or guidance.
- Believe success is a one-time achievement rather than a lifelong process.

World-Class Achievers:

- Prioritize constant learning and self-improvement.
- Surround themselves with mentors, coaches, and peers who challenge them.
- See every experience as an opportunity for growth.

How to Apply This:

- Dedicate time daily to reading, courses, or skill development.
- Join mastermind groups or find mentors in your industry.
- Challenge yourself to adopt new perspectives and unlearn limiting beliefs.

6. Managing Energy, Not Just Time

Average Performers:

- Focus on time management without considering energy levels.
- Work in long, unproductive stretches, leading to burnout.
- Ignore physical and mental well-being.

World-Class Achievers:

- Align tasks with peak energy periods for maximum efficiency.
- Prioritize sleep, exercise, and mental recovery as key success factors.
- Use strategic breaks to sustain focus and creativity.

How to Apply This:

- Identify your most productive hours and schedule high-focus tasks accordingly.
- Use techniques like The Pomodoro Method to maintain energy balance.
- Treat recovery (sleep, nutrition, movement) as non-negotiable.

7. The Ability to Stay Focused in a Distracted World

Average Performers:

- Constantly switch tasks, leading to shallow work and poor results.
- Allow notifications, emails, and social media to hijack their focus.
- Struggle to commit to deep, meaningful work.

World-Class Achievers:

- Create distraction-free environments that foster deep work.
- Set clear boundaries around communication and digital usage.
- Train their minds for long periods of sustained focus.

How to Apply This:

- Implement time-blocking for deep, focused work sessions.
- Remove distractions using website blockers and phone-free zones.
- Practice mindfulness and meditation to enhance focus and mental clarity.

Why Discomfort Is Your Greatest Advantage

Embracing Discomfort for Growth

Most people spend their lives avoiding discomfort. They seek the path of least resistance, choosing comfort over challenge, ease over effort. Yet, the truth is that discomfort is the gateway to growth. Every major breakthrough—whether in business, sports, or personal development—happens when individuals step outside their comfort zones and willingly embrace discomfort.

Discomfort signals that you are stretching beyond your current limits, pushing into new territory, and expanding your capacity for success. High performers don't fear discomfort; they seek it out. They understand that growth and comfort cannot coexist, and they use discomfort as a strategic tool to sharpen their skills, build resilience, and reach new levels of achievement.

This chapter will explore why discomfort is not something to be feared, but rather a powerful advantage—one that, when harnessed, can set you apart from the majority and catapult you toward excellence.

1. The Biology of Discomfort: Why We Resist It

The human brain is wired for survival, not for growth. Our evolutionary programming prioritizes safety, routine, and predictability, because historically, staying in familiar territory increased the chances of survival. However, this same instinct now works against us in the modern world, where success demands adaptability, learning, and continuous improvement.

The Science Behind Discomfort:

- The Brain's Threat Response: Discomfort triggers the amygdala, the part of the brain responsible for processing fear and threats.

- Neuroplasticity and Growth: Pushing through discomfort rewires the brain, making challenging tasks easier over time.
- Hormonal Shifts: Stress, when managed correctly, leads to the release of dopamine and endorphins, which reinforce the reward of overcoming challenges.

Instead of avoiding discomfort, high performers train themselves to reframe it as a necessary signal for growth.

2. The Link Between Discomfort and Success

Every significant achievement in history has been built on stepping into discomfort. Whether it's an entrepreneur taking a financial risk, an athlete training through exhaustion, or an artist pushing creative limits, greatness is forged in moments of struggle.

How Discomfort Drives Success:

- Resilience: Facing challenges repeatedly strengthens mental toughness.
- Learning Acceleration: New skills and experiences are acquired faster under pressure.
- Fear Conditioning: Regular exposure to discomfort reduces fear and increases confidence in tackling the unknown.

Example: Elite athletes train beyond their comfort zones daily. They push their physical and mental limits, conditioning themselves to thrive under stress. The same principle applies to business and life—those who embrace discomfort become leaders in their fields.

3. How to Leverage Discomfort as an Advantage

Discomfort is a tool, but only if you learn to lean into it instead of retreating from it. Here are some strategies to turn discomfort into a competitive edge.

1. Reframe Discomfort as Growth

Instead of seeing discomfort as something to be avoided, view it as a sign of progress. When something feels hard or unfamiliar, it means you're developing a new capability.

2. Develop the Habit of Voluntary Discomfort

Deliberately exposing yourself to controlled discomfort builds resilience and mental toughness.

- Cold showers to build physical resilience.
- Public speaking challenges to overcome social fear.
- Physical training beyond perceived limits to push endurance.

3. Commit to the 10% Rule

Increase the difficulty of your tasks by just 10% beyond your comfort zone. This small stretch ensures consistent progress without overwhelming resistance.

4. Seek Feedback and Criticism

Most people avoid feedback because it's uncomfortable. But the fastest way to grow is through constructive feedback. Ask for input regularly and use it to refine your skills.

5. Embrace Failure as a Learning Tool

Failure is simply data—a source of valuable insights. Instead of fearing failure, analyze it, adjust, and improve. The most successful people fail frequently because they are always pushing their limits.

4. The Long-Term Benefits of Embracing Discomfort

By consistently stepping into discomfort, you create a long-term advantage over those who choose comfort and safety. Here's what happens when you train yourself to embrace discomfort:

- You Become Fearless: Fear loses its power when you confront it regularly.
- You Build an Adaptability Edge: You become more flexible in navigating uncertain environments.
- You Outperform the Competition: Most people avoid discomfort, giving you a natural advantage in growth and execution.

Summary: The Scaling Effect

Elevating Execution to the Next Level

Execution is the foundation of success, but true mastery comes from scaling your ability to perform at a high level consistently. The Scaling Effect is about amplifying focus, accountability, and mindset to not just maintain progress but accelerate it over time. High performers don't settle for marginal improvements—they develop systems that enable exponential growth.

Mastering Focus in a Distracted World

Distractions are the biggest killers of deep work and meaningful progress. To truly scale performance, focus must be intentionally cultivated. This means eliminating digital and mental clutter, creating an environment that supports deep work, and mastering the art of saying no to non-essential commitments. When focus becomes a priority, execution becomes unstoppable.

Leveraging Accountability and Feedback

Self-discipline alone isn't enough to sustain high-level execution. Accountability is the missing link between goals and results. By building a Topify Circle of accountability—surrounding yourself with people who challenge, support, and push you—you eliminate excuses and create continuous momentum. Public and private commitments add another layer of reinforcement, ensuring that actions align with aspirations.

Thinking Like a High Performer

Elite execution is not just about doing more—it's about thinking differently. High performers adopt a mindset of resilience, relentless learning, and extreme ownership. They differentiate themselves by embracing discomfort as a tool for growth, constantly refining their approach, and viewing challenges as stepping stones to greater success. Scaling performance is a mindset as much as it is a strategy.

The Scaling Effect in Action

By implementing these principles—focused execution, structured accountability, and an elite mindset—success becomes inevitable. Scaling is not about working harder; it's about working smarter and strategically compounding small wins into significant breakthroughs. When focus, accountability, and mindset align, progress accelerates exponentially.

Part 5: The Legacy

Beyond Success—Building a Legacy

Success is not just about achieving goals; it's about creating lasting impact. Productivity, focus, and execution mean little if they don't lead to something meaningful. Legacy isn't built on what you do—it's built on how your actions shape the world around you.

The final stage of mastering the Topify Method is understanding how to turn productivity into purpose, ensuring that your efforts align with your values and leave a lasting imprint. This is where personal growth meets contribution, and where high performance becomes about more than just personal gain—it becomes about scaling impact beyond yourself.

The Transition from Productivity to Purpose

Many people chase success only to find themselves feeling unfulfilled. Why? Because productivity without purpose feels hollow. The key to sustained motivation and long-term success is aligning your actions with a greater mission. In this section, you'll explore how to transform daily execution into meaningful progress that benefits both you and those around you.

The Topify Challenge: The Next Step in Mastery

Mastering the Topify Method doesn't stop with understanding its principles—it requires implementation. The Topify

Challenge is a 90-day execution plan that reinforces everything you've learned and pushes you to your next level. Through structured tracking, reflection, and refinement, you'll gain clarity on your personal path to high performance while ensuring that your productivity serves a greater purpose.

What You'll Learn in This Section:

- How action fuels fulfillment and the connection between productivity and purpose.
- Designing a life that aligns with your values, so success feels meaningful.
- Scaling your impact beyond personal success, creating a ripple effect of positive change.
- The Topify Challenge—a structured 90-day plan to solidify the method in your life.

The true power of execution lies in its ability to shape a meaningful future. This section will help you move from being productive to being purposeful, ensuring that your actions not only create success but also leave a lasting legacy.

Chapter 12: Turning Productivity into Purpose

Beyond Productivity—Finding Meaning in Action

Productivity is often seen as a means to an end—a way to check off tasks, hit targets, and maximize efficiency. But true fulfillment comes when productivity is connected to a deeper purpose. Working harder or getting more done is not enough; the real question is: Are you spending your time on things that truly matter?

Many high achievers fall into the trap of relentless execution, only to find themselves burned out and unfulfilled. The missing piece? Aligning daily actions with a meaningful purpose. When productivity is driven by purpose, every task, decision, and goal becomes part of a bigger picture—one that fuels motivation, deepens satisfaction, and creates lasting impact.

The Shift from Task-Oriented to Purpose-Driven Work

Most productivity systems focus on efficiency—how to get more done in less time. While this is valuable, the real transformation happens when you shift from simply being busy to being intentional. Purpose-driven work means prioritizing actions that align with your values, aspirations, and long-term vision.

This chapter will explore how to move from productivity for productivity's sake to a life of meaningful execution. You'll learn how to connect daily habits to your larger mission, ensuring that every action contributes to a legacy worth building.

What You'll Learn in This Chapter:

- How action fuels fulfillment—why meaningful work leads to greater satisfaction.
- Designing a life that aligns with your values—defining success on your own terms.
- Scaling your impact beyond personal success—turning productivity into influence and contribution.

The goal is not just to do more—it's to do the right things with purpose and intention. This chapter will help you redefine productivity so that it serves a higher mission, creating success that is both measurable and meaningful.How Action Fuels Fulfillment

The Link Between Action and Purpose

Fulfillment is not found in passive reflection or wishful thinking—it is created through intentional action. Many people believe they must first discover their purpose before taking action, but in reality, action itself is what reveals purpose. When we engage in meaningful work, pursue challenges, and take deliberate steps toward our goals, we experience a sense of progress, contribution, and satisfaction.

High achievers understand that fulfillment is not a destination but a process—one that is built through consistent, purpose-driven execution. By taking action aligned with your values, you create a life of meaning, impact, and deep satisfaction.

1. The Myth of Waiting for Purpose

Many people believe they need to first uncover their passion or purpose before they can take meaningful action. This leads to stagnation, overthinking, and inaction. However, the reality is that purpose emerges through action.

Why Waiting for Purpose Is a Mistake:

- Clarity comes from doing, not thinking.
- Passion is developed, not discovered.
- Progress fuels motivation, not the other way around.

Example: An entrepreneur doesn't wait to feel fully ready before starting a business—they take action, learn, and refine their mission along the way. The same applies to anyone looking for meaning in their career, relationships, or personal growth.

2. The Science Behind Action and Fulfillment

Studies show that people who actively pursue goals and engage in meaningful activities experience higher levels of happiness, fulfillment, and well-being.

Key Psychological Principles:

- The Progress Principle: Even small progress on meaningful work leads to greater life satisfaction.

- Dopamine and Achievement: Taking action and achieving milestones releases dopamine, reinforcing motivation.
- Flow State: Engaging in deep, purposeful work creates a state of immersion and fulfillment.

How to Apply This:

- Set daily micro-goals that contribute to your larger vision.
- Reflect on progress rather than just outcomes.
- Engage in work that challenges and excites you.

3. How Small Actions Lead to Big Meaning

Taking action doesn't always mean making life-changing decisions. Small, consistent efforts accumulate into massive impact over time.

Examples of Purposeful Action:

- Volunteering for a cause you care about.
- Mastering a skill that allows you to contribute to others.
- Mentoring or teaching others from your own experiences.

How to Apply This:

- Identify 1-3 small but meaningful actions you can take daily.
- Prioritize consistency over intensity—small steps create momentum.

- Look for ways to integrate purpose into your existing work and habits.

4. The Role of Service in Fulfillment

One of the greatest drivers of fulfillment is helping others. Studies show that people who contribute to something beyond themselves experience greater life satisfaction.

Ways to Serve Through Action:

- Building a business that solves real problems.
- Creating content that inspires or educates.
- Supporting a community or cause that aligns with your values.

How to Apply This:

- Ask yourself: *Who can I help today?*
- Shift your focus from personal gain to value creation.
- Take action in ways that positively impact others.

Designing a Life That Aligns with Your Values

Living with Intention

Many people go through life reacting to circumstances rather than intentionally shaping their path. They take on commitments, careers, and lifestyles that feel expected rather than choosing those that truly resonate with their core beliefs.

However, real fulfillment comes from designing a life that aligns with your values—not society's, not your family's, but your own.

A values-aligned life provides clarity, purpose, and deep satisfaction. It ensures that your daily actions contribute to something meaningful, rather than just keeping you busy. In this chapter, we'll explore how to identify your core values, align your daily actions with them, and create a blueprint for a purpose-driven life.

1. Identifying Your Core Values

Before you can align your life with your values, you need to define what truly matters to you. Your values act as a personal compass, guiding decisions and priorities.

Steps to Identify Your Core Values:

1. Reflect on Peak Experiences – Think about moments in your life when you felt truly alive. What themes emerge?
2. Assess What Makes You Frustrated or Unhappy – Often, when something deeply bothers us, it's because it conflicts with our values.
3. Look at Your Heroes – The people you admire can provide insight into the values you aspire to uphold.
4. Ask the Big Questions:
    - What kind of impact do I want to make?
    - How do I want to be remembered?
    - What principles do I refuse to compromise on?

Example Values: Integrity, Growth, Freedom, Contribution, Creativity, Connection, Excellence, Adventure.

2. Aligning Your Actions with Your Values

Once you have clarity on your core values, the next step is to ensure that your daily actions reflect them. Many people experience stress or dissatisfaction because they live out of alignment with what truly matters to them.

Practical Strategies for Value Alignment:

- Audit Your Life: Identify areas where your current lifestyle, work, or relationships conflict with your values.
- Create a Values-Based Decision Framework: Before committing to something, ask, *Does this align with my values?*
- Prioritize What Matters Most: Dedicate time and energy to activities that reinforce your values while eliminating distractions.
- Say No More Often: If an opportunity, project, or relationship doesn't align with your values, have the courage to walk away.

Example: If one of your core values is freedom, but your job feels restrictive and uninspiring, it may be time to explore more flexible career options or side projects that align with your deeper purpose.

3. Designing Your Ideal Day and Lifestyle

A values-aligned life isn't built overnight—it's crafted one day at a time. The way you structure your daily habits determines whether you stay true to your values or drift away from them.

How to Build a Daily Routine That Reflects Your Values:

- Start with Morning Intention-Setting: Define your top priority for the day based on your values.
- Use the 80/20 Rule: Spend 80% of your time on activities that align with your values and eliminate the rest.
- Establish Boundaries: Protect your time from obligations that don't align with your bigger vision.
- Reflect and Adjust: At the end of each day, review whether your actions were aligned with your values and make micro-adjustments as needed.

Example: If one of your values is personal growth, set aside daily time for reading, learning, or skill development. If connection is important, prioritize meaningful conversations over mindless scrolling on social media.

4. Overcoming Challenges and Staying Aligned

Living in alignment with your values is not always easy. You'll face external pressures, self-doubt, and difficult decisions that test your commitment.

Common Challenges and How to Overcome Them:

- Societal Expectations: Many people feel pressure to follow a traditional path. Remind yourself that your life is yours to design.
- Fear of Change: Making adjustments to align with your values may require difficult shifts, such as changing careers or leaving toxic relationships. Embrace discomfort as part of growth.
- Short-Term Temptations: Opportunities that bring immediate rewards may not always align with your long-term values. Stay disciplined in making choices that serve your bigger vision.

Strategy for Staying Aligned: Schedule regular personal check-ins—quarterly or annually—to reflect on whether you're staying true to your values and adjust as needed.

Scaling Your Impact Beyond Personal Success

The Shift from Personal Success to Lasting Impact

Success is often measured by personal achievements—career milestones, financial security, and personal growth. However, true fulfillment comes when we scale our impact beyond ourselves, influencing and empowering others. The most successful individuals don't just accumulate wealth or recognition; they create systems, communities, and legacies that uplift people and drive meaningful change.

Scaling impact means moving from individual accomplishments to leveraging skills, knowledge, and resources to create a ripple effect. Whether through leadership, mentorship, philanthropy, or innovation, expanding your influence ensures that your work leaves a lasting imprint.

1. The Mindset Shift: From Personal Gain to Collective Growth

Many people focus on personal success but fail to recognize that real significance comes from contribution. High-impact individuals understand that helping others grow amplifies their own success.

How to Shift Your Mindset:

- Redefine success: Instead of only measuring personal milestones, track how many lives you positively influence.
- Embrace abundance thinking: View opportunities as limitless and recognize that sharing success does not diminish your own.
- Ask: Who can benefit from what I know or have? Whether it's knowledge, experience, or resources, your impact multiplies when shared.

2. Mentorship: Empowering Others Through Knowledge

One of the most powerful ways to scale impact is through mentorship. Sharing your expertise accelerates the growth of others, helping them navigate challenges more effectively.

Ways to Become an Effective Mentor:

- Formal mentorship programs: Join or create structured mentorship groups within your industry.
- One-on-one mentoring: Offer guidance to aspiring professionals or individuals seeking direction.
- Content creation: Write, speak, or create resources that reach a larger audience beyond direct mentorship.

Example: Many successful entrepreneurs create courses, books, or podcasts to share lessons they've learned, impacting thousands instead of just a few.

3. Leadership: Creating Systems for Sustainable Impact

Scaling impact requires moving beyond individual effort to leading and building structures that outlast you. Whether in business, nonprofit work, or community initiatives, great leaders create frameworks that empower others to thrive.

Key Strategies for Impactful Leadership:

- Delegate and empower: Teach others to lead rather than micromanaging tasks.
- Build a high-performance culture: Foster environments where growth, innovation, and impact thrive.
- Think beyond your presence: Structure teams and systems that operate effectively even when you're not directly involved.

Example: A business owner who mentors and develops leaders within the company ensures that their vision continues to grow beyond their personal efforts.

4. Philanthropy and Social Responsibility

Success is most meaningful when it contributes to solving bigger problems. Philanthropy and giving back are essential components of scaling impact beyond personal success.

Ways to Contribute:

- Financial giving: Supporting charities, nonprofits, or funding education programs.
- Volunteering: Offering time and expertise to causes that align with your values.
- Corporate social responsibility: Integrating impact-driven initiatives within your business or organization.

Example: Entrepreneurs like Bill Gates and Oprah Winfrey have used their success to fund initiatives in healthcare, education, and social justice, creating long-term impact.

5. Building a Legacy: Making an Enduring Contribution

A legacy is more than wealth or recognition—it's about leaving something meaningful for future generations. True legacy-building involves creating sustainable structures that continue to create impact long after you're gone.

How to Build a Meaningful Legacy:

- Document and share your knowledge: Write books, create content, or establish training programs.
- Build organizations that last: Whether it's a business, nonprofit, or movement, design something that operates beyond your direct involvement.
- Develop future leaders: Invest in the next generation by mentoring and empowering emerging leaders.

Example: Figures like Nelson Mandela and Mother Teresa built legacies not through personal achievement alone, but by empowering others to carry forward their work.

Chapter 13: The Topify Challenge

The Ultimate Test of Execution

You've absorbed the principles of high performance, execution, and purpose-driven productivity. Now it's time to put it all into action. The Topify Challenge is not just another goal-setting framework—it's a 90-day execution plan designed to push you beyond your limits and create lasting transformation.

Success isn't built on theory; it's built on consistent, intentional action. The Topify Challenge is a structured approach to ensuring that the strategies in this book aren't just ideas but become embedded in your daily life. By committing to 90 days of focused execution, you'll solidify habits, strengthen discipline, and unlock a new level of performance.

Why 90 Days?

Research shows that 90 days is the optimal period for significant personal transformation. It's long enough to create meaningful change but short enough to maintain momentum. Over the next three months, you will track progress, refine your execution strategies, and build a system that sustains success long after the challenge is complete.

What to Expect in This Chapter:

- How to implement the Topify Method for 90 days with structured daily and weekly execution.

- How to use the Topify Scorecard to track performance and refine habits.
- The mindset shifts required to unlock the next level of your life.

This is where everything you've learned comes together. Are you ready to commit, take action, and see what's truly possible when you execute with precision and purpose?

Implementing the Topify Method for 90 Days

Turning Knowledge into Action

The difference between those who achieve extraordinary results and those who remain stuck is not intelligence, talent, or even motivation—it's execution. The Topify 90-Day Challenge is designed to take everything you've learned and put it into structured, intentional action. Over the next three months, you will transform how you operate daily, creating habits and systems that sustain long-term success.

A 90-day commitment forces you to shift from short-term effort to long-term consistency. It eliminates hesitation, builds momentum, and allows for measurable progress. This is not a passive challenge—it's a deep commitment to excellence, discipline, and personal mastery.

Step 1: Setting Clear, Measurable Goals

The first step in implementing the Topify Method for 90 days is defining exactly what success looks like. Your goals must be specific, measurable, and outcome-focused.

How to Set Your 90-Day Goals:

1. Identify Your Core Objective – Choose one primary focus area for the next 90 days (business growth, health transformation, personal development, etc.).
2. Break It Down into Milestones – Set monthly and weekly targets to track incremental progress.
3. Use the Topify Scorecard – Track daily execution and reflect on progress weekly.
4. Define Non-Negotiable Habits – Commit to daily and weekly habits that align with your goals.

Example: Instead of saying, "I want to get in shape," set a goal like: "I will work out five times a week and reduce my body fat by 5% in 90 days."

Step 2: Structuring Your Days for Maximum Execution

Success is built in the details of your daily execution. The Topify Method emphasizes structured time management to remove decision fatigue and enhance focus.

The Daily Execution Plan:

- Morning Review: Start each day by reviewing your Top 3 Priorities.

- Time Blocking: Schedule dedicated action blocks for deep work.
- The 80/20 Focus: Spend 80% of your time on high-impact activities.
- End-of-Day Review: Reflect on what worked, what didn't, and what adjustments need to be made.

Step 3: Weekly Refinement and Course Correction

Every week, you will analyze progress, remove inefficiencies, and optimize execution. Weekly reflections allow you to adapt instead of blindly pushing forward without awareness.

The Weekly Review Process:

1. Assess Your Scorecard – What percentage of your goals were met?
2. Identify Patterns – What's working? What's slowing you down?
3. Refine Your Strategy – Adjust your action plan based on real data.
4. Recommit with Clarity – Set clear priorities for the next week.

Step 4: Maintaining Energy and Mental Resilience

Sustaining high performance for 90 days requires energy management and mental resilience. Burnout is the enemy of execution.

Key Strategies for Maintaining Momentum:

- Prioritize Sleep and Recovery – Your brain and body need rest to operate at peak performance.
- Stay Accountable – Engage with a Topify Circle or mentor.
- Use Micro-Resets – When you hit resistance, use short resets (deep breaths, movement, journaling) to regain focus.

The Topify Scorecard

Measuring What Matters

The Topify Scorecard is the ultimate tool for tracking execution, refining strategies, and ensuring continuous improvement. Many people set ambitious goals, but without a system to measure progress, motivation fades and results suffer. The Scorecard eliminates this uncertainty by providing a clear, data-driven framework to assess daily, weekly, and monthly performance.

What gets measured gets managed. By consistently using the Topify Scorecard, you'll gain insights into what's working, what needs adjustment, and how to sustain peak performance over the long term.

1. The Structure of the Topify Scorecard

The Scorecard is built on three key tracking levels:

- Daily Execution – Ensuring that every day aligns with your core goals.

- Weekly Progress Review – Identifying trends, challenges, and areas for refinement.
- 90-Day Reflection – Evaluating the long-term impact of your actions.

Each level serves a distinct purpose, reinforcing discipline, focus, and adaptability.

2. Daily Execution: Tracking High-Impact Actions

Success is built one day at a time. The Daily Scorecard focuses on execution consistency, ensuring that the most critical tasks get done.

How to Use the Daily Scorecard:

- Top 3 Priorities: Write down the three most important tasks for the day.
- Action Block Completion: Mark whether you dedicated focused time to deep work.
- Energy & Mindset Check-In: Rate your energy levels and mindset on a scale from 1-10.
- End-of-Day Reflection: Assess what went well, what could be improved, and key takeaways.

Example Daily Scorecard Entry:

Date	Top 3 Priorities	Action Blocks Completed	Energy Level (1-10)	Key Takeaways
Jan 1	Finish report, client call, gym	3/3	8	Strong focus, need better morning routine

By maintaining daily tracking, you stay accountable to your commitments and develop self-awareness about what drives success.

3. Weekly Progress Review: Refining Execution

The Weekly Scorecard review allows you to zoom out and analyze patterns. It helps identify what's working, where momentum is building, and where adjustments are needed.

Key Weekly Metrics:

1. Task Completion Rate: What percentage of your daily Top 3 tasks were completed?
2. Execution Consistency: How many days did you stick to your action plan?
3. Biggest Wins & Lessons Learned: Identify breakthroughs and obstacles.
4. Adjustments for the Next Week: What needs to be improved or optimized?

Example Weekly Summary:

- Task Completion Rate: 85%
- Execution Consistency: 6 out of 7 days
- Biggest Win: Deep focus improved due to time blocking.
- Adjustment: Reduce distractions in the afternoon.

4. 90-Day Reflection: Evaluating Long-Term Impact

After 90 days, the Topify Scorecard serves as a performance audit, revealing your strengths, growth areas, and future opportunities.

Key 90-Day Reflection Questions:

- What were my biggest accomplishments?
- What habits contributed most to my success?
- Where did I struggle, and why?
- What changes will I implement for the next 90 days?

This process ensures that execution evolves over time, keeping you on a trajectory of continuous improvement.

Unlocking the Next Level of Your Life

The Path to Your Greatest Potential

Reaching the next level of your life isn't about working harder—it's about working with greater clarity, precision, and purpose. It requires breaking through the mental and physical barriers that keep you stuck in familiar cycles. The Topify Method has provided you with the tools to execute at a high level, but true transformation comes when you use those tools to elevate not just your productivity, but your entire way of thinking, operating, and living.

The next level is not a destination—it's a process of continuous evolution. This chapter will explore how to push beyond self-imposed limits, adopt an elite mindset, and create an environment where success becomes inevitable. Whether in your career, personal life, or mission, unlocking the next level means taking control of your trajectory and executing with intention.

1. Identifying What Your Next Level Looks Like

Before you can reach the next level, you need to define what it means for you. Most people stay stuck because they lack clarity on what they're striving toward. Without a clear vision, effort becomes scattered and results remain inconsistent.

How to Define Your Next Level:

- Identify the Gap: Where are you now vs. where do you want to be?
- Clarify Key Areas: What aspects of your life need the biggest shift? (Career, health, relationships, impact)
- Set a High-Resolution Goal: Instead of vague ambitions, set specific, measurable targets.
- Visualize It Daily: Mentally step into the identity of the person who has already reached that level.

Example: Instead of saying, *I want to be more successful*, define it as: *I will increase my business revenue by 50%, optimize my personal health, and establish a stronger leadership presence within 12 months.*

2. The Mindset Shift: Operating from a Higher Standard

Your mindset determines your level of execution. If you continue operating with the same beliefs, habits, and patterns, you will get the same results. Unlocking your next level requires shifting your mindset to think, decide, and execute like a high performer.

Key Mindset Shifts:

- From Passive to Proactive: Stop reacting—start setting the pace.
- From Excuses to Ownership: Drop self-limiting beliefs and take full responsibility for outcomes.
- From Fear to Confidence: Lean into discomfort and take bold action before you feel ready.
- From Consistency to Precision: Optimize actions, eliminate inefficiencies, and refine execution.

How to Apply This:

- Surround Yourself with High Performers: Your environment dictates your standards.
- Develop an Elite Routine: High performers design their days around peak energy and deep work.

- Commit to Relentless Growth: Never stop learning, refining, and leveling up.

3. Building Systems That Sustain Long-Term Growth

Momentum isn't created by working harder—it's created by working smarter. To stay on a trajectory of continuous growth, you must implement systems that sustain high performance.

Core Systems for Unlocking the Next Level:
1. The Topify Scorecard: Tracking progress ensures accountability and refinement.
2. The 90-Day Execution Cycle: Working in focused cycles prevents stagnation.
3. The Environment Optimization Method: Design a workspace and lifestyle that naturally supports success.
4. Accountability Structures: Leverage mentors, peer groups, or personal coaches to maintain high standards.

Example: Instead of just relying on motivation, a high performer creates structured work blocks, automated decision-making (e.g., meal planning, workout scheduling), and weekly performance reviews to maintain progress.

4. Pushing Past Resistance and Unlocking Flow

Every level comes with resistance. Fear, doubt, and external challenges will arise—but those who consistently push beyond resistance achieve breakthroughs.

How to Push Through Resistance:

- Recognize Resistance as a Sign of Growth: If it feels uncomfortable, you're expanding.
- Use Micro-Actions to Create Momentum: Instead of overthinking, start small and build up.
- Master the 45-Second Reset: When resistance strikes, reset quickly and refocus.
- Tap Into Flow States: Remove distractions, fully immerse in tasks, and work in deep-focus cycles.

Example: A leader facing imposter syndrome doesn't retreat—they take immediate, bold action, reinforcing confidence through execution rather than hesitation.

5. Scaling Your Impact: Elevating Beyond Yourself

The highest level of success isn't just about personal growth—it's about making an impact. The more you elevate, the more you can contribute beyond yourself.

How to Scale Impact at the Next Level:

- Mentorship: Teach and guide others on their journey.
- Leveraging Teams & Delegation: Focus on what only you can do and empower others to execute.
- Building a Legacy: Whether through business, philanthropy, or thought leadership, extend your influence.
- Creating Systems That Outlast You: Set up structures that continue generating results without constant effort.

Example: A high performer who has mastered personal productivity doesn't stop there—they build a community, write a book, or create a system that empowers others to succeed.

Summary: The Legacy

Elevating Productivity into Purpose

Part 5 of the Topify Method shifts the focus from personal execution to lasting impact. While the earlier sections built the foundation of high performance, this final part is about ensuring that your productivity serves a greater mission. The highest achievers don't just focus on themselves—they create systems, influence others, and leave a legacy that continues to grow beyond them.

Turning Productivity into Purpose

Success without purpose leads to burnout and dissatisfaction. This section highlights how action fuels fulfillment by aligning daily efforts with deeper values. Designing a life around what truly matters ensures that productivity isn't just about checking off tasks but creating meaningful results. Scaling impact beyond personal success means mentoring others, leveraging leadership, and making contributions that extend your influence beyond the immediate.

The Topify Challenge: The 90-Day Execution Plan

The Topify Challenge is a structured 90-day plan that pushes you to implement everything learned in this book. It reinforces discipline, execution, and refinement. Through the Topify

Scorecard, you measure progress, analyze what's working, and optimize for better results. The challenge is about mastering habit-driven success and proving that small, consistent actions lead to massive breakthroughs.

Unlocking the Next Level

Reaching your next level isn't just about working harder—it's about thinking bigger, refining systems, and continuously pushing past resistance. This section encourages you to operate from a higher standard, embrace discomfort as a catalyst for growth, and scale impact by mentoring, delegating, and building lasting structures that multiply your influence.

The Final Shift: From Productivity to Legacy

The final step in mastering execution is ensuring your work leaves a lasting impact. Whether through business, leadership, or personal growth, true success is measured not just by what you achieve but by how many others you empower. The Topify Method is not just about getting things done—it's about transforming how you execute, lead, and create change that lasts well beyond you.

Your Future Starts Now

The Power to Create Change

The journey through the Topify Method has been about more than productivity—it has been about unlocking your highest potential. You now hold the framework, strategies, and systems to take control of your time, energy, and execution. But the real transformation begins when you decide to apply what you've learned. Knowledge without action changes nothing. Your future is shaped by what you do today, and this final section is your invitation to step fully into the life of purpose, productivity, and impact you were meant to lead.

High performers aren't born—they are built through intentional action, relentless refinement, and an unwavering commitment to growth. This book has given you the blueprint, but it's up to you to execute.

This closing section will recap the core principles of the Topify Method, invite you to join a movement of driven individuals, and show you how to seamlessly integrate the Topify Productivity Planner into your daily routine to sustain your momentum. The only thing standing between where you are now and the future you envision is consistent execution. The time to start is now.

What's Next?

- A recap of the Topify principles so you can internalize and apply them daily.

- The invitation to join the Topify movement, where like-minded individuals commit to high-performance living.
- How to use the Productivity Planner for maximum results, turning strategy into daily execution.

This is not the end of your journey—it's the beginning of something greater. The next level of your life is waiting. Are you ready to step into it?Recap of the Topify Principles

The Power of Intentional Execution

The Topify Method is more than a productivity system—it is a philosophy for structured action, continuous growth, and meaningful success. Throughout this book, we have explored the frameworks and habits that separate high performers from those who struggle with execution. Now, as you prepare to integrate these principles into your daily life, let's revisit the core foundations that make the Topify Method so powerful.

Success isn't about working harder; it's about working smarter, with precision, and unwavering clarity. Mastering these principles will allow you to take control of your time, energy, and output, ensuring that every action you take aligns with your highest goals.

Principle 1: Clarity Over Chaos

High performers don't guess—they operate with crystal-clear focus. Clarity drives action, eliminates distractions, and ensures that every effort contributes to meaningful outcomes.

- Define your big vision with measurable goals.
- Use the Topify Vision Framework to turn abstract ideas into structured execution.
- Prioritize high-impact tasks instead of reacting to low-value distractions.

By focusing on clarity, you eliminate the uncertainty that leads to procrastination and inefficiency.

Principle 2: Structured Action Beats Raw Effort

Most people believe working harder leads to success, but without structure, effort becomes wasted energy. The Topify Method is built on systems that streamline execution and optimize performance.

- Break goals into actionable steps using the Reverse Engineering Model.
- Utilize the 90-Day Sprint Approach to sustain focus and momentum.
- Leverage time-blocking and execution cycles to ensure maximum productivity.

Success isn't random—it is the byproduct of deliberate, well-structured action.

Principle 3: Mastering Prioritization for Maximum Impact

Being busy is not the same as being productive. True success comes from focusing on what truly moves the needle.

- Use the Topify Quadrants to categorize tasks into Essential, Growth, Delegation, and Elimination.
- Ensure your daily execution aligns with your Top 5 Priorities, focusing on your Top 1 first.
- Develop the discipline to say no to low-value tasks, eliminating distractions that dilute your progress.

Prioritization is the key to consistently making meaningful progress instead of drowning in tasks that don't matter.

Principle 4: Habit Stacking and Sustainable Execution

One-time effort doesn't create lasting results—consistency does. The Topify Method integrates habit stacking to ensure execution becomes second nature.

- Build non-negotiable daily routines that reinforce high-performance habits.
- Leverage momentum by committing to small, repeatable wins every day.
- Use the compound effect of small actions to create exponential growth.

Sustained success is not built on motivation—it's built on disciplined execution.

Principle 5: Overcoming Resistance and Procrastination

Even the most disciplined individuals face resistance. The key is knowing how to push through and execute, even when motivation is low.

- Understand the psychology of procrastination and remove barriers to action.
- Rewire your brain for execution using micro-commitments and quick wins.
- Use the 45-Second Reset to instantly shift from hesitation to action.

Winners don't wait for motivation—they create it through action.

Principle 6: Tracking and Refining Progress

What gets measured gets improved. The Topify Method emphasizes continuous tracking and refinement to ensure sustained high performance.

- Use the Topify Scorecard to track daily execution and identify patterns.
- Conduct weekly reviews to refine strategies and optimize efficiency.
- Evaluate 90-day execution cycles to sustain long-term momentum.

By regularly analyzing progress, you prevent stagnation and ensure that every phase of execution leads to measurable growth.

Principle 7: Scaling Beyond Personal Success

High performance isn't just about personal achievement—it's about scaling your impact beyond yourself.

- Mentor and empower others, sharing the principles of execution.
- Leverage systems and automation to maximize results with minimal effort.
- Think like a legacy builder, ensuring your work has lasting influence.

The highest level of success is not just about winning for yourself—it's about creating a ripple effect that transforms others.

The Invitation to Join the Topify Movement

The Power of a Collective Mission

Success is rarely achieved in isolation. While individual execution is essential, the most sustained and impactful growth happens when like-minded people come together with a shared purpose. The Topify Movement is built on this idea—a community of high achievers, doers, and visionaries who are committed to structured action, personal mastery, and creating meaningful impact.

The journey you've undertaken through this book has equipped you with the tools to transform your approach to productivity, mindset, and execution. But the real challenge is not in learning these principles—it's in sustaining them over the long term. That's where the Topify Movement comes in. It's an ecosystem designed to provide support, accountability, and continuous growth so you can maintain momentum and keep evolving.

This isn't just about being more productive—it's about living with purpose, clarity, and relentless execution. Now, you're invited to join a network of high performers, entrepreneurs, leaders, and action-takers who are all committed to leveling up, not just in their personal success but in their ability to create lasting impact.

Why a Movement? Why Not Just a System?

A system can teach you how to execute, but a movement amplifies your ability to execute consistently. When you surround yourself with people who hold you to higher standards, challenge your thinking, and push you to be better, you elevate far beyond what you could achieve alone.

The Benefits of Being Part of the Topify Movement:

- Accountability & Support: Stay on track with a community that keeps you committed.
- Access to New Insights: Learn from experts, peers, and high achievers who share strategies and experiences.

- **Momentum & Motivation:** Being surrounded by driven individuals keeps your energy and execution levels high.
- **Opportunities for Collaboration:** Connect with like-minded professionals to scale your impact beyond personal success.

Execution isn't just about knowing what to do—it's about continuously evolving and pushing your limits. The Topify Movement provides the structure and environment to make that growth inevitable.

How to Get Involved in the Topify Movement

1. Commit to the Topify Execution Standard

The foundation of the movement is a commitment to relentless execution. Joining isn't about consuming more knowledge—it's about taking action. Members embrace the Topify Principles and hold themselves accountable to the highest standard of performance.

2. Engage with the Topify Community

This isn't just about reading a book—it's about joining a global network of high achievers who are applying these principles every day. Engaging with the community gives you access to:

- Weekly challenges that push execution to the next level.
- Live Q&A sessions and mastermind groups.
- Resources, case studies, and real-world applications of the Topify Method.

3. Leverage the Productivity Planner & Scorecard

To ensure execution remains consistent, members of the movement integrate the Topify Productivity Planner and Scorecard System into their daily routines. This structured approach keeps focus sharp and execution measurable.

4. Participate in the 90-Day Topify Challenge

One of the most powerful ways to solidify your habits is through the 90-Day Topify Challenge. This structured program helps you apply everything in this book with real-time accountability and measurable progress tracking.

The Future of Topify: Scaling Beyond Personal Success

The goal of the Topify Movement isn't just individual success—it's about creating a collective impact that goes beyond personal achievement. High performers lead by example, and as part of this movement, you have the opportunity to:

- Mentor and support others who are on their journey to mastery.
- Contribute insights and lessons learned to help refine and strengthen the system.
- Build businesses, initiatives, and projects that create impact beyond yourself.

Turning Strategy into Execution

The Topify Productivity Planner is more than just a tool—it's a daily execution system designed to ensure consistent, high-performance action. Many people fail to reach their goals not because they lack ambition, but because they lack a structured way to execute. The Productivity Planner eliminates guesswork, helping you prioritize, track progress, and optimize execution.

To fully integrate the Planner into your life, you must develop the habit of daily planning, structured prioritization, and reflection. This chapter will walk you through how to use the Planner effectively, ensuring that every day moves you closer to your biggest goals.

1. The Core Structure of the Topify Productivity Planner

The Planner is designed around the principles of the Topify Method, which emphasizes clarity, structured action, and continuous improvement. Its layout is simple yet powerful:

Key Components:

- Daily Execution Framework: Focuses on Top 5 Priorities, with an emphasis on the Top 1 that must be completed.
- Time Blocking System: Schedules deep work sessions to maximize productivity.
- Progress Tracking: Includes a daily scorecard to measure execution and refinement.
- Reflection & Refinement Section: A space for end-of-day reviews to optimize future performance.

By following this framework consistently, you eliminate distractions, enhance focus, and drive execution at the highest level.

2. The Morning Routine: Setting Up for Success

Your morning routine is the launchpad for a productive day. Integrating the Productivity Planner into your morning ensures that you start each day with clarity and focus.

Morning Planning Steps:

1. Review Your Long-Term Vision: Keep your big goals in mind to ensure alignment.
2. Identify Your Top 5 Priorities: Select five key tasks that drive meaningful progress.
3. Highlight Your Top 1 Non-Negotiable Task: This is the task that must be completed no matter what.
4. Schedule Action Blocks: Assign dedicated time slots for deep work.
5. Set an Intention for the Day: A simple focus statement to guide your mindset.

This process ensures that every day is structured for success before distractions take over.

3. The Execution Phase: Sticking to the Plan

Planning means nothing without consistent execution. The Productivity Planner helps you stay on track by keeping your priorities visible and ensuring structured action throughout the day.

Execution Best Practices:

- Follow Your Time Blocks Relentlessly: Treat scheduled work sessions like unmissable appointments.
- Use the 45-Second Reset: When you feel stuck, reset quickly and re-engage.
- Eliminate Distractions: Keep the Planner open as a constant reference to stay focused.
- Check Off Completed Tasks: This small action reinforces progress and builds momentum.

By sticking to your daily execution framework, procrastination fades and momentum builds.

4. The Evening Review: Refining and Optimizing

The end-of-day review is where transformation happens. By reflecting on what worked and what didn't, you ensure that each day becomes a stepping stone toward greater success.

Evening Review Steps:

1. Score Your Execution (1-10): Rate your overall effectiveness for the day.
2. Analyze What Worked Well: Identify habits and strategies that drove success.
3. Assess Challenges & Distractions: Note what slowed you down and how to mitigate it.

4. **Set the Next Day's Priorities:** Prepare your Top 5 so you start strong the next morning.

Daily refinement ensures that you're not just working hard, but working smarter every day.

5. Long-Term Execution: The 90-Day Sprint

Consistency compounds over time. The Productivity Planner is built for 90-day execution cycles, ensuring that short-term focus leads to long-term transformation.

The 90-Day Integration Process:

- Week 1-4: Develop Planner habits and refine execution.
- Week 5-8: Optimize time-blocking and eliminate inefficiencies.
- Week 9-12: Scale execution by increasing challenge and complexity.

After 90 days, review your progress and set the next sprint, ensuring sustained success.

Your Next Step: Take Action Now

You've made it to the end of *The Topify Method*, but this is just the beginning. Reading about productivity and execution won't change your life—**taking action** will. Now, it's time to put everything you've learned into motion.

Get the Topify Productivity Planner

The best way to implement The Topify Method is to have a structured system that keeps you focused, accountable, and making progress every day. That's exactly why I created the Topify Productivity Planner—a simple, powerful tool to help you:

- Break down your goals into daily, actionable steps
- Track your progress over 90-day sprints
- Eliminate distractions and focus on what truly matters
- Build momentum with structured reflection and planning

Get your Topify Productivity Planner now at topifymethod.com/planner

Stay Connected & Keep Growing

This journey doesn't end here. Surround yourself with people who are also taking action and living the Topify way. Join the Topify community to:

- Get exclusive insights and productivity tips

- Connect with **like-minded high achievers**
- Receive **ongoing support** to keep you accountable

Your Challenge: Commit to 90 Days

Change doesn't happen overnight. But in **90 days**, you can completely transform how you work, think, and execute. Right now, **write down one big goal you will commit to for the next 90 days.**

My 90-Day Goal:_____
My First Action Step: _____

Now, take the first step. Don't wait for the "perfect time"—start today. **Every great achievement begins with the first move.**

Help Others—Share Your Journey

If this book has helped you, the best thing you can do is **pay it forward.**

- **Share this book** with someone who needs it.
- **Leave a review**—your feedback helps others discover The Topify Method.
- **Tag me on social media** and share your journey using #TopifyMethod

Thank you for being part of this movement. **Now go out there and execute.**